WHAT IS
CREATIVITY?

Kevin Jan Bonner.

For Debs.

CONTENTS

INTRODUCTION.

Halfway through writing this book, I realised I had been composing it in my head for most of my life. For decades, I had been making uncertain, disparate observations about creativity that needed tidying up and sewing together. I'd been trying to make sense of this niggling 'thing' that kept cropping up: this nagging discontent about the way creativity has always been misunderstood and misrepresented.

It appeared to me that no one had a cohesive and comprehensive understanding of the subject. Every time I heard someone talk about creativity, or write about it, these feelings of dissatisfaction were reinforced. There was always an anomaly, a disagreement, and sometimes just plain disbelief at the way commentators and 'experts' described this essential human quality.

Whenever I had one of these jolts of discontent, I registered another thought, idea or discrepancy. Finally, after years of frustration, these irritations and incongruities have bubbled to the surface – forcing me to action.

So here it is– in three parts – a definitive answer to the question, what is creativity?

This is not a dry scientific treatise, but a book of personal observations and thoughts – all of them originating from my experiences of observing creativity, living with creativity and attempting to teach it.

1

In the process, I blow away the traditional smog of misunderstanding and mystery, revealing a lucid and complete model. A model that answers all of the questions. A model that is capable of standing up to the rigours of interrogation and analysis.

****

I have been involved with creativity all of my life. At school I was told I was talented in the visual arts. Consequently, I pursued an arts education in the British art school system.

There, I learnt art skills: how to draw, paint, print, sculpt, take photographs and make films – how to think about art, and how to make art. I followed courses. I took exams. I hung around with other 'creative' people. I dallied and I dabbled. I learnt to 'talk the creative talk' and 'walk the creative walk'.

When I left art college, I used my knowledge and skills to set up a craft and design business. I made large sculptural wooden toys as well as furniture and other bespoke items.

As the business expanded, I employed people. I sold my products worldwide, and I won awards for them. During this process, I engaged with business people and advisors: bankers, apprentices, employees, dealers – and, of course, the general public.

Many promoted creativity as the panacea for personal achievement, a healthy lifestyle, a successful business, a strong nation and worldwide happiness.

In the evenings I taught 'Art and Craft' subjects to adults. Many of my students claimed they wanted to be more creative. They wanted to do creative things as an antidote to their uncreative day jobs.

To complement my teaching, I wrote books on craft subjects. I illustrated the books and took photographs for them.

I continued to be creative, often in very practical areas of my craft business that traditionally would not be thought of as requiring creativity.

Eventually, I trained to be a teacher. I used creativity to improve my teaching, plan lessons, and design curriculums of study.

I became the head of an Expressive Arts Faculty. I taught art, design, drama and music. I tried to get others to understand creativity and work creatively. I observed what motivated creativity, and– just as importantly– what stopped it.

Outside of school I lingered with all sorts of other projects. I have always enjoyed exploring new creative ventures, and I have been fascinated with the process by which these ideas manifest themselves. In particular, how creativity can be developed or smothered.

I have had ideas for: board games, internet sites; proposals for film scripts, and novels. I have devised new products, and services: edible sandwich wrappings, perpetual motion engines, insomnia cures. The depth and range of my interests have been extensive.

Some ideas were attempted and failed. Some succeeded for a while before fading. Some remained as silly ideas, and some are still waiting to be developed. All were creative.

In short, I have spent most of my life immersed in creativity: talking about it, doing it, absorbing it, being puzzled by it, being excited by it, watching it, living it – learning to keep afloat in the often cold and choppy waters – swallowing, flapping, choking, kicking.

Occasionally I have moved with elegance. More frequently, with the grace of an overly large man wrapped in seaweed.

Over the years I have become deeply sensitised to creativity. In particular, with the anomalies and incongruities surrounding the subject.

I have recognised creativity in many non-traditional places: in the jokes and banter with friends and strangers, in the attempts to relieve the boredom of unskilled work, when playing sports and games, in the activities of young children and the behaviour of students.

I have used creativity in excuses and explanations, in arguments, cooking and conversations. I have observed creativity in the ways that my children, and now my grandchildren, pick their way through their lives, employing and rejecting creativity.

I have identified that creativity can be identified at many levels: from the mildly interesting throwaway line of a passing conversation, to the brilliant idea that solves a once insuperable problem.

But how is this possible?

We are taught from an early age that creativity is a rare and capricious beast that only gifted and talented people can tame. How can creativity appear in so many places, to so many people, and at so many levels?

Just as importantly, I recognised the absence of creativity in areas of life that were usually the epitome of ingenuity and the very beacon of creativity: dreary design, soporific writing, pointless inventions, lack-lustre films, stale television programmes. Traditionally, these are the places we should all find creativity. How could this be?

Perhaps creative people are not creative all the time? But then what causes creativity to be turned on... and turned off? Why are, so-called, creative people at times bereft of creativity? Or, as often observed, creative in one part of their lives but dull and very ordinary in other parts?

Why are some people immensely creative for a few short years or months before apparently losing the ability – quickly returning to the obscurity of an ordinary life?

Where did they go wrong... or right?

What perverse mechanism drives this creativity? There are so many unanswered questions. In an attempt to find the answers, I have researched and enquired widely, with little satisfaction.

All I got was more problems to add to the list: more confusion, more quandary, more niggling questions, more nagging doubts.

But why should I be looking for someone else to answer these questions? I have spent my whole life surrounded by traditional notions of creativity. Surely, after a lifetime of saturation in this most watery of subjects, I should have acquired the answers.

After all, if I had spent a career in any other occupation – even if I had not paid too much attention, or had been looking the wrong way at the time – I would have absorbed an acceptable grounding in the fundamentals. Surely, by now I should be proficient in the basics of creativity. Then it happened.

One fine flawless morning I came up for air and inhaled deeply. The reason I am still searching for answers – and the reason creativity is such an arcane and puzzling subject – is because no one really understands it.

My mind cleared. I saw with new eyes. I realised: not once, in this inspired, lifelong immersion – not once, in this life of learning, creating and teaching – had I undergone any lessons, training, debate or lecture that instructed, questioned, explored, explained or even touched upon the subject of creativity.

Furthermore, in a whole career involved with 'creative' subjects, I cannot think of one occasion when creativity was talked about with more than dismissive platitudes.

I do have sinking memories of trying to initiate discussions about creativity with fellow students, tutors, teachers and other professionals. I remember lofty suggestions to investigate certain people and to read particular books.

6

Never did my research match my experience of creativity, satisfy my curiosity, or answer my questions.

Some claimed creativity is not supposed to be understood. They said it was an individual thing – a bit like religion, questionable politics or personal hygiene – not to be talked about in polite company. These claims were often accompanied by an off-stage supine stare that quickly led to a disagreement about the most fundamental platforms for discussion....

"What is creativity?"

"How can we identify it?"

"How can we define it?"

"How can we measure it?"

Chins would be rubbed, faces pulled, and heads scratched. But rarely did the conversation get any further. You quickly learn in creativity circles that creativity is not a subject for serious discussion.

Then another slug of fresh air ushered in a new thought. If I am looking for the truth about creativity – a truth that answers all the difficult questions, with all the boxes ticked – I am going to have to do it myself, by drawing upon my own empirical experiences and my own research.

And, if I wanted any help grasping the depths and breadth of creativity or understanding the essential ingredients there would be no point asking the creative professionals.

If my lifetimes experience of creativity had shown one thing it was that 'creative people' were just as ignorant to the workings of creativity as everybody else. Today's, so called, 'creative experts' still tinker around the edges of the old fashioned, muddled model of creativity that has been in place for centuries.

But this is an amazing declaration. These people are at the centre of this frenzied maelstrom: in the eye of the storm. These people are supposed to talk, walk, eat, drink and sleep the subject. Most had graduated through an education system focussing on a creative subject. Presumably they are more creative than average. You may imagine they would have acquired a smattering of knowledge about this essential behaviour. Or, at the very least, be able to provide a credible description.

Obviously, there must be something wrong here.

Looking back, it is incredible:

It's like Police Officers not talking about crime,

Doctors not discussing medicine,

Chefs not speaking about food.

How is this possible?

It seems creativity has always been the thought behind the action,

the silence between the notes,

the canvas behind the painting,

the unspoken word – essential but unrecognised.

8

But why are we all so ignorant of this most vital of subjects?

We understand the atomic structure of the universe. We understand how the human body works, and we know the recipe for lemon drizzle cake. Incredibly, all these things we understand **because** of creativity, but we do not understand the behaviour that causes these amazing things. The structure, detail and scope of this phenomenon is a mystery to us all. Yet we live with it – day-in, day-out.

Civilisations, cities and cultures are founded and flounder on the use, misuse and misunderstanding of creativity.

Even after tens of thousands of years, Mankind cannot define creativity with agreement or simplicity. We do not have the vocabulary to dissect and discuss this most important of subjects; we do not know how it works, how to identify it, how to teach it, how to generate it, or how to assess it.

At best, it is a vague abstract notion; at worst, it is a mediaeval mystery. Most worryingly, we are not aware of this misunderstanding and the damage our ignorance can cause.

If we are to find answers to the vast problems of our age, we are going to find them using the great engine of creativity.

But if creativity is an engine of change, should we not take an active interest in how the mechanism works, and how we might get the best performance from it?

If we are going to rely on creativity to make changes, should we not – in this highly charged, nuclear age – consider the benefits and consequences of those changes?

9

Over the millennia the creativity engine has become more and more powerful: once it was a rusty two-stroke, just capable of 'putt-putt-putting' over the savanna; today it is a shiny roaring jet capable of blasting us all into space Shouldn't we be able to apply the brakes when it is not needed? Shouldn't we be able to teach our children what this machine looks like, and how to control it?

Creativity has brought us careering down the millennia; like wild-eyed extras in some demented science fiction film: hurtling, skidding, crashing, braking – and currently accelerating into the future. But here is the big question. Where will it end? Where is this mad, malevolent, magnificent machine going to deposit us?

If we could understand the mechanism. If we could adjust the controls. Perhaps we could enhance the possibilities and limit its dangers. Maybe we could draw a map and discuss our destination. Perhaps, in our wildest imaginings... we could steer.

So, here is the importance of understanding creativity: if we do not comprehend this thing, if we cannot identify it, if we do not have the language to talk about it, if we cannot play with it, if we cannot pull it apart and reassemble it, if we do not feel comfortable in its presence – then we cannot improve it, we cannot develop it, we cannot teach it.

Creativity will always be a universal mystery, dragging us by the nose into an uncertain future.

THE CHASE.

Mankind is forced to chase its tail,

always obliged to seize that branch–just out of reach.

Our restless troubled species spirals into a dark future

looking for something that cannot be found.

The virtuous circle has become a vortex:

sucking everything, helter-skelter, into its eye–

searching for harmony, just beyond our grasp.

We are building a new world with our creativity,

without a plan, without a vision, without a map.

This is our future:

The unknown.

kjb.

PART ONE.

TRADITIONAL VIEWS OF CREATIVITY.

Our present-day traditional understanding of creativity is a hodgepodge of many different ideas tacked together over thousands of years into a patchwork muddle.

In this first section of the book, I explore this confusion of blurred views. I pull them apart and examine them to see if they have any value in our new understanding of creativity.

1.1 DOMAINS OF CREATIVITY.

There is no commonly agreed definition of creativity. Creativity is a nebulous term with many interpretations and descriptions. The immense variety of them is testament to its legacy of imprecision.

Certainly science does not have an answer. Although, in the second half of the twentieth-century research into creativity increased, we still do not have a clear definition that we can all agree upon. A simple search of the internet for a definition of creativity exposes many pages of very interesting and sometimes perplexing interpretations. Some are simple and curt; many are long-winded and complex. All leave questions and doubts.

Often, the contributions seem to bathe in the imprecision of the subject. It's as if we are all entitled to wax lyrical, allowing anybody that feels the urge to make a florid stab at the subject.

It's as if creativity is meant to be a vague notion– on the edge of our understanding – like a dark vacuum that sucks in any passing opinion or half-brewed notion.

Some claim there are over a hundred definitions of creativity. Well, even if we acknowledge a dozen of those to have merit that is eleven too many. Creativity is too important a subject to park in this fug of disagreement – guessed at, ruminated upon, and squinted over.

We need a much firmer understanding to light our way. We need a solid definition of creativity we can all use. But where do we start?

The traditional notions of creativity are riddled with ancient inconsistencies, misunderstandings and distorted meaning. If we are going to construct a new understanding of creativity, we need to lay new foundations. But before we discard the old beliefs and traditional concepts, we should take a close look at them. We need to examine these time-honoured ideas that many have grown to accept. It would be foolish to throw them out without consideration; some of them might contain helpful information.

I do not intend to examine each definition or viewpoint, there are far too many for that. However, it would be worthwhile to examine some of the most popular ideas, so we can expose, examine, dispel or accommodate them.

ART DOMAINS.

Perhaps the most widespread and common idea about creativity is that it is confined to small areas of human activity. These are often referred to as 'domains. The domains that are most often linked to creativity are associated with the practice of an art.

This collection of domains has a long tradition of producing creative products: sculpture, crafts, design – work within the theatre or film industries – painting, advertising, certain types of writing, dance, music and photography.

For centuries, activities that were linked to 'The Arts' have been an unquestioned home of creativity. However, the idea you are being creative just by being involved with an artistic pursuit is impossible to sustain.

In my experience of teaching the arts – and my involvement in their production – uncreative art is far more common than the creative type. We could make an argument that to be involved in these arts domains we are trying to be creative. This is more sustainable. In addition, we could say the purpose of an artistic activity is to be creative. These claims may be worth a closer look in later chapters. Whatever the intention, we must accept these artistic domains are just as capable of producing uncreative products as any other field of human endeavour.

Undoubtedly, we could claim there is a higher percentage of creativity in these artistic areas of life in comparison to other domains, such as fly-fishing or driving a taxi. Perhaps we could reason that by involving yourself in an 'arts subject' you have a higher likelihood of being creative, or by making arts and crafts you are expected to be creative. But just taking part in a particular art activity is no guarantee you will behave creatively or that you will produce creative products.

There is more to creativity than turning up with your musical instrument, your paint box, or your dancing shoes, and expecting everything you do to be creative.

Creativity is more than making art, and it is more than taking part. Making art is not dependent upon being creative, and creativity is not dependent upon being artistic.

Therefore, we cannot reference the artistic domains in our new definition or our new understanding of creativity. There is a strong link, but the link is not firm enough or exclusive enough.

TECHNOLOGY.

What about the domain of technology?

Many claim this area of life to be brimming with creativity. In popular culture, inventors, boffins and technicians are the personification of a certain type of creativity. Particularly in the computer age with new hardware, software, websites, games and 'apps' appearing on a daily basis.

Popular culture would cite this place as the home of creativity. Surely, the creators of new technology are creative: they are making the future before our very eyes.

Undoubtedly, they are... sometimes. But we would be hard-pressed to sustain a claim for technology as the fountain of creativity on this basis.

Technology has a long history of dour conformity with existing principles that should not be breached. Consequently, we can find just as much uncreative behaviour in technological circles as there is in any other domain.

We can see creativity in there somewhere, but we need to look beyond our computer screens and flashing gadgets for a more satisfying and comprehensive understanding of creativity.

BUSINESS.

How about the domain of business? Perhaps this is where creativity should be defined? What could be more creative than making money, providing jobs, building business empires?

18

Many claim that this is the place creativity resides: new cars, refrigerators, publications, financial products. All of these, and many millions more, are created each year to satisfy the popular lust for the next new product.

Each new creation drives our economies.

Each is the result of someone's hard work and enterprise.

And certainly, in many of them we can discern creativity.

But you only have to look around the shops to see that most businesses deal with unoriginal merchandise filling unadventurous needs.

Yes, there is creative stuff in there – sitting on top of the boring, commonplace essentials. Certainly, we all clamour to have our bank accounts tickled by the new, the innovative, the fresh – and we pay a premium for it.

But most of the time we take home the predictable, the dependable and the known.

Business might claim that it strives for creativity, but its best-seller is the safe, the staid – the uncreative.

MEDICINE.

What about the most worthy domain of all: medical science?

Anybody unfortunate enough to need the facilities of a hospital will realise the wonders of creativity a modern hospital provides: the instruments to measure, the tools to prod and poke, the diagnoses, the medicines, the surgical procedures – all the products of creativity.

19

The creative mind focused on medicine is constantly dreaming up new procedures, new drugs and new treatments – for the body and the mind: saving and improving our lives, solving our endless medical problems, salving our wounds, soothing our tortured existences.

Helping us to survive longer and better is a good description of what medicine does.

Could this be the basis for a definition of creativity? Surely, developing new medical procedures and improving lives is the most important creative act. But does creativity have to be important? Does creativity need to save lives to be of value?

Can't it also be found in the glib comment, the rash decision, the hastily drawn cartoon, even the unfinished.......

ENTERTAINMENT.

Many consider the world of entertainment is where we should locate a definition of creativity. At first sight, this whole domain is devoted to and reliant upon innovation and originality. Entertainment is focused on keeping our novelty hungry minds occupied through numerous industries of creative behaviour.

Surely, this has to be the home of creativity in its purest form: new songs, stories, dances, films, music, shows and sports. The range of Mankind's creativity in the domain of entertainment is phenomenal. Consequently, we can see that creativity is fundamental to the domains of entertainment.

But is entertainment the heart and soul – the guts – of creativity?

Isn't entertainment just the candle on the creativity cake?

Isn't creativity much more vital?

Surely, humanity did not become the most powerful species on this planet, fighting its way against trillions of insatiable competitors, over billions of years, by being able to sing, dance and tell a few jokes.

Obviously, creativity has a lot to do with entertainment, but entertainment can't be what made human beings such voracious competitors of evolution.

Of course, creativity is here, but it has to be the chrome plating, not the 24-carat stuff that clawed humanity from the caves to the stars.

We cannot define creativity solely as a preserve of entertainment. However, we have to admit that entertainment is an important facet of human creativity, and we can understand a lot about creativity through its examination.

Consequently, later I shall be examining the relationship between entertainment and creativity in more depth.

SCIENCE.

If we cannot anchor creativity in the domain of entertainment, how about science? A popular conception of creativity lives in the idea of the mad scientist: wide gleaming eyes, unkempt hair, smoking test tube in hand; mixing up the next abomination that could wipe out humanity with the accidental push of a button, or save the planet from itself – depending on which film you watch.

Closer to reality is the idea of the scientist as the plain old researcher looking for a solution to the common cold, or a new type of chewing gum.

Some consider this the real place contemporary Mankind creates: in the pristine laboratory, surrounded by blinking machines; bleach-coated tedium, patiently chipping away at a tiresome problem, making our lives better a pipette drop at a time.

It does not sound like a very exciting view of creativity. Is this where we are to locate the most important and influential attribute of humanity? Surely, we can find a better example for our definition – and a better characterisation.

Science is arguably the most creative area of human endeavour: dissecting the universe. So why do we not applaud its creativity? Why does popular culture characterise the scientist as the contrarian of creativity: a plodding pedant – addicted to data?

Scientists take the greatest show on earth – drawing back the curtains of the universe – and they present it as a trawl through facts and figures, all done with the most laudable and very necessary intentions.

Now, I am not saying science is boring – far from it – it is just that most of the time that is how Mr and Mrs Public perceive the processes and the personnel involved.

How can we define creativity, the most exciting and vital characteristic of Mankind, as something steeped in the scientific status quo?

It would not be fair to define creativity as scientific enquiry. Perhaps it is a very good contender, but we need a more comprehensive and more exciting example to guide our way.

ART MARKET.

I have already argued against the creative domains of 'The Arts', but there is one aspect of art that has long been thought of as being the home of creativity in popular culture, so it deserves a special mention: Contemporary Art. Many people think that if any area of modern life has a claim on creativity it has to be this one.

In the world of contemporary art, the idea of creativity is central to its purpose. Creativity – that elusive commodity – is the ultimate unique selling point. It enables art to be sold to patrons and collectors in the definitive sales pitch. Whole panjandrums of ideas become rammed into the singular quality of creativity. Ideas such as genius, refinement, sensitivity, goodliness, godliness, elitism, artistry, mystery, spirituality, exclusivity, rarity and originality. All these, and more, are packaged and sold as part of the contemporary art commodity.

These superlative human qualities are proclaimed in an effort to raise the price of artworks along with the significance and indefinable 'creative genius' of the artist. Finding and claiming creativity, then making money from it, is the **business** of the Art World. Herein lies the clue.

The contemporary art world is a business. A business that sells creativity. Of course, some contemporary art displays a lot of creativity, but much of it is cliched and over-hyped. In addition, sometimes its financial value is based on other factors, such as skill, rarity, economics, entertainment value and notoriety – not on creativity.

The problem for the layperson, or anyone else, is discerning which is which? What is creative? What is skilled? What is rare? What is good art? What is bad art? Generally, the prices paid for contemporary artwork are out of the reach of the average person, so the contemporary art domain exists as a plaything of the rich.

All well and good–if it stays that way. But often the contemporary art market becomes the arbiter of what is good or bad art, collectable and uncollectable, valuable and worthless – and more particularly for us – creative and uncreative.

The contemporary art world filters society's artistic domains removing anything it considers undesirable. Unfortunately, in that filter is caught an enormous amount of artistic creativity incapable of turning a big enough profit for the dealer.

There is nothing wrong with this as a structure of the domain, or as a business model, as long as we are all aware of this bias and these filters.

For those that understand the rules, the art market can be very entertaining. However, when the contemporary art world becomes the judge of what is creative and what is not creative, parading itself as the home and well-spring of creativity, it does us all a disservice.

The contemporary art market is full of amazing objects, and it displays all sorts of human characteristics – one of them being creativity. But this particular creativity is tainted and twisted by a market focused on profit. Therefore, it would be incorrect to link our new definition to the contemporary art market, or for it to be referenced in our new understanding.

In all these claims for creativity, in all these domains – and many more – we can see creativity has a claim to be there. Creativity *appears* in all these domains, but it does not sit comfortably or exclusively in any of them. We cannot define creativity by claiming it is located in an individual domain. Wherever we look we can find creativity– often in the most unlikely of activities.

When we examine domains for creativity, what we really find is our ignorance, our misconceptions and our misunderstandings.

Besides, even if we wanted to put an individual domain on a creativity plinth, these domains are not exclusive: they cross over and collide with one another. Where does the art stop and the entertainment begin? Where is the line between business and technology? Technology, medicine and science could all be part of the same 'super' creative domain.

In our new definition and our new understanding, we cannot locate creativity in one discrete area of human activity.

Creativity is far too important and effervescent for that.

Our definition has to position creativity as part of all our lives, and recognised as part of all domains.

1.2. CREATIVE PROCESSES.

In their efforts to understand creativity, many observers focus on the behaviour renowned 'creative people' use when being creative. These are the mythical 'creative processes' some commentators talk of. They can contain several stages. Here is a common one, much used in the design 'domains'.

Identify: find and refine a problem.

Research: gather information.

Incubate: allow the information to be assimilated.

Generate: find ideas that solve the problem.

Implement: choose the best idea and use it.

Review: evaluate and assess the result.

There are a number of variations on this procedure. Some are more convoluted and detailed than others. Some observers claim this is what successful creative people do – intuitively.

Some claim the use of these processes can teach creativity to 'uncreative' people. Others believe that the use of these processes can lead to more and better creativity.

These procedures are sometimes referred to as 'process scaffolding'.

This sort of activity breaks down a complex behaviour into a number of smaller, easier to deal with operations.

By carefully completing each action those attempting to be creative ensure no part of the work is missed, and that each stage is given due attention.

In addition, when the work is over the person trying to be creative can return to analyse and improve any unsatisfactory parts of their work.

However, just as scaffolding in real life does not build the house for you, the scaffolding process does not supply the creativity. You still have to make decisions prompted by the process. It is in those decisions and subsequent behaviour that the creativity is located – not the scaffolding.

There is no guarantee that the use of the scaffolding framework will lead you to a – metaphorically – creative building. Using this process, you could end up with a castle or a coal bunker, or a conventional house – just like every other house on the street.

Creativity is more sophisticated than this.

Like any series of behaviours these scaffolding methods are only as good as the decisions taken at each stage.

The scaffolding process can be useful when teaching students to think about a problem and its possible solutions, but it does not solve the problem for you. And the scaffolding framework will not, by itself, make anyone more creative.

Without a broader understanding of creativity– particularly knowing what creativity is – these processes are just as likely to compound the ignorance and add to the confusion.

The simplest creative process consists of two parts: divergent and convergent thinking. Once again, some claim this is the natural behaviour of 'creative people'.

In essence, divergent thinking expands the number of possible solutions we can apply to a problem – this is the first stage. The second stage – convergent thinking – aims to choose the best answer from the array of solutions uncovered in the first stage.

Once again, there is some merit in their use, but the argument against the scaffolding process still stands. This process is only as good as the judgements and decisions made when using the framework. Creativity is a lot more than generating lots of ideas or solutions.

This process can produce hundreds of different ideas in the divergent stage – all of them could be uncreative. If we do not understand what creativity is, or know what creativity looks like, we may never find a creative idea to converge upon.

Reducing creativity to a series of simpler actions then applying a reductive process can have some value in certain domains and particular situations. However, this sort of deconstruction process it is not enough to guarantee creativity or help our understanding of it.

We need to understand creativity at a much deeper level and appreciate it on a much broader scale before this sort of process can be beneficial.

1.3. TESTING FOR CREATIVITY.

In the twentieth century, some scientists tried to test for 'natural creative ability'. One traditional assessment asks the candidates to find as many uses as possible for an everyday object, such as a brick.

Apparently, the more uses the participant could find for the brick the more naturally creative that person was thought to be.

In theory, this process will provide a numerical measurement of the person's divergent thinking – therefore, their innate creativity. However, once the participant takes these tests, they can quickly learn the criteria for success and the types of responses that improve their score. Consequently, they can get much better at playing the game and their results improve.

In this way, the tests do not measure the assumed inborn creativity of a person. They record the experience of the person being tested with the rules of the game.

You can very quickly learn how to improve your divergent thinking scores just by practising the techniques. Just as you can learn to improve your success at chess, billiards or poker, by playing the game frequently and studying the inherent structures.

There is another difficulty with this method of improving or assessing innate creativity. It may be applied to a single 'stand-alone' problem or an individual problem reasonably easily: how to improve sales, what subject to paint, where to go on holiday.

These sorts of scaffolding processes can get the brain ticking over and focused. However, they are difficult to apply to other domains that present themselves as collections of problems: designing a city, writing a concerto, painting a landscape or eye surgery.

All of these tasks are collections of problems. In these examples, each line, note, cut or stroke is a problem that needs a solution. Some activities can involve thousands of decisions – some of those decisions might be creative.... some not.

Theoretically, it would be possible to identify each problem in the activity and analyse them discretely. However, to apply a tortuous creative process to each individual action, then expand the number of divergent thoughts, before converging on a creative solution, would be extremely tiresome, very debilitating and unfeasible to perform – or assess.

Furthermore, in some domains problems are launched in quick succession such as sports, playing a musical instrument, or wrestling an alligator. It would be impossible to stop the major activity and apply irksome processes to ensure a creative response to each minor action.

Once again, we see that creativity reveals itself to us in many different ways.

Creativity can be tested for, but first we need to understand exactly what we mean by creativity, and what makes one act of creativity better than another. These questions shall be answered in later chapters.

1.4. PRETEND AND AUTHENTIC CREATIVITY.

Many factors influence the behaviour of a person, especially when they are trying to be creative. For example: motivation, skills, knowledge and confidence.

Other influences include the type of problem being set and the way it is presented. And, of course, the domain of the problem can greatly affect the outcome.

But undoubtedly, the biggest influence is the seriousness of the problem to the person attempting to be creative.

Because we are all unique, we each have our own view of what is a serious problem and what is a successful solution. We can play games with creativity, and we can form mock problems to test how well we play those games, but this leads to Pretend Creativity.

If I am not particularly interested in playing those pretend games, or if I am cynical about the aims of the game, I will not take them seriously, or care whether I am very good at them.

****

On the other hand, Authentic Creativity deals with serious and genuine problems of the individual located in a real-life situation. This sort of problem is difficult to replicate in a test because the problems of the unique individual are often private, even subconscious.

Often the motivation to be creative is as unique as the person. Authentic Creativity is personal and meaningful. It is focused on serious problems that are really important to the individual.

Authentic Creativity is only invoked when a person encounters a challenge that really affects them, and when they are determined to solve a problem.

Our most vital and serious creativity is reserved for our most vital and serious problems.

For example: it makes sense that a boxer would save their best performances for their toughest fights. You would not expect a boxer to fight as if their life depended upon it every time they get into a ring. Their performance would depend on who is being fought and what they are fighting for.

Similarly, you would not expect a poet to produce their finest work if they were feeling indifferent and unmoved by a subject.

If we had tested Mozart's creativity by asking him to make a creative cake, I suggest he would probably have made a mess of it.

And, if we had asked Shakespeare to paint a creative still-life, I am sure he would not have known where to start.

If the problem belongs to someone else, we are unlikely to take it seriously and employ our unique personal creativity.

Authentic Creativity is embedded in the time and environment it is performed in and in the inimitable character and problems of the people attempting to be creative.

Shakespeare and Mozart made creative products that were important to them and concerned them as individuals. Their creativity was as individual as they were and as unique as the times they were created in.

From this, we can see that creativity varies in its strength. That strength depends on the seriousness of the problem we encounter and how much of a challenge the problem presents us.

We can also see that setting tests using 'pretend creativity' misunderstands the true nature of creativity.

1.5. THE WORDS OF CREATIVITY.

There are many words that have become associated with creativity; many of them are misleading or confusing.

Some people think of creativity as a verb: as a synonym for 'making'. This view suggests that whenever we make anything we are being creative.

By this understanding, if we were to make, construct or assemble: a meal, a garden, a cake, a story, a piece of artwork, a tree-house or an excuse, we are being creative. No matter how the final product turns out, so the thinking goes, if you are in the process of making you are creating.

This is possibly the most mundane and down-to-earth idea about creativity I have encountered; however, its simplicity does creativity an injustice.

By these terms, anything and everything we make or do can be described as creativity: any design, any birthday card, any building, any story– just by baking bread we are being creative.

Under this idea, there is no requirement for the creativity to produce anything special, or solve a problem, or be a thing of beauty, or for the creative behaviour to have discovered some new scientific truth.

Creativity as a 'catch-all' verb undersells it. This notion is just *too* simple. It does not expose the full range of its qualities or the complexity it inherently possesses.

Creativity is about making things, but it is about making things that have specific and special qualities. Standing on an assembly line making the commonplace, or copying somebody else's work, can, in certain circumstances, be creative – but generally, it is not. Therefore, creativity as a verb that represents all forms of making, is not precise enough, and it has to be rejected from our new understanding.

****

Many definitions describe creativity using common adjectives: original, innovative, new, unique, valuable, inventive, novel, different. The idea that creativity can be described, or even defined, by using the above words is very common.

Let's examine some of them.

ORIGINAL.

Yes, creativity does exhibit originality, but so do many other things.

Take the thirteenth word from each page of Tolstoy's *'War and Peace'* and you will have an original radio play. If you were to intersperse each sentence with noises of the sea and flashing lights, it would be a very original radio play. It would also be very annoying to listen to. In addition, it would be unintelligible. Some may describe it as creative, but there are many other terms better suited.

I have never cut my toenails with a chainsaw – does this mean this behaviour is original and therefore creative? How do we decide what is original and what is not?

Originality depends on the context. If I have never made a lemon drizzle cake before, then the behaviour would be original to me – but it would not be original to many thousands of other people that have done it many times before.

Original behaviour for one person may be boring and cliched to another. *Anything* that an individual, or group of people, has not done before can be described as original.

INNOVATION.

Many commentators champion creativity in the guise of innovation. This is particularly true in the world of business. Innovation is often claimed to be the answer to our economic ills. Business leaders, around the world, claim innovation and creativity are the top requirements for growth and success. But innovation cannot be the same as creativity, and it cannot be relied upon to engender creativity.

Throwing a pot of paint over the C.E.O. is innovative, but it is unlikely to improve profits – or gain you promotion. Including a live cockroach with every box of soap powder, would be extremely innovative, but it would be unlikely to increase sales or 'lift the bottom-line'. Kicking the ball to your goalkeeper every third pass is unique and extremely innovative, but it would not win the game.

If we were to write about failed innovative businesses, we could fill a hundred libraries detailing their plight. Yet business gurus and commentators rely on innovation, in the guise of creativity, as the touchstone for business success. What do they mean?

If our economic future is dependent upon creativity and innovation, and we cannot define these factors, is it any wonder we so often find ourselves in dire fiscal circumstances?

IMAGINATION.

Using the imagination and being imaginative suggests a particular form of thinking that involves playing speculatively with ideas and images.

I can imagine the moon is made out of chocolate, that the world is flat, or at some time in the future we shall be able to travel through time. I am using my imagination. I am being imaginative; however, as you may have noticed, I have not been original or creative.

In fact, all thinking uses imagination. The most humdrum thinking relies upon our imaginations. Which way shall I walk to work? Shall I have tea or coffee? What film shall I watch? Who shall I vote for?

All of these questions involve considering potential behaviours, imagining a solution, and choosing the best one. However, we would not normally call this workaday process 'being creative'.

As we have seen previously, this process is sometimes called divergent and convergent thinking.

Certainly, creativity involves using the imagination – but so do most other behaviours. It is possible to be imaginative and not be creative. Consequently, it is confusing and inaccurate to define or describe creativity as 'thinking imaginatively'.

VALUE.

Some observers claim creativity has to have value. However, value is a subjective and unstable term.

We know from economics that a stale loaf of bread is priceless in a famine but worthless at a feast. An abstract painting in a garage sale, or dustbin, has very little value. But the same painting on the walls of a world-renowned gallery, spoken about in hushed tones by leading supporters in the art world, can generate enormous sums of money.

Objects can, and do, have their values inflated or deflated by external factors. The stock markets of the world are wonderful examples of this with fortunes being won and lost on changing values.

Besides, there are so many ways something can be valued: apart from the financial and aesthetic, we can value something for its simplicity, its complexity, its cheapness, its respect for the environment, its heritage, its ability to make someone laugh, cry or think – its popularity, its rarity, its colourfulness, its utility.

Furthermore, creativity can have a value to the individual, but it can have a different value to the community, or the species.

Which value do we use when judging or defining creativity?

All of these values, and many more, can be invoked in our *evaluation* of creativity – but we cannot use them to define or assess it.

In addition, some of our most conventional, boring, unoriginal, unimaginative behaviours and objects are of enormous value to us. Where do they fit into this idea?

If these old-fashioned uncreative properties can have value – what value is value in our definition?

Unquestionably, creativity can be of colossal value, but it can also be worthless – even a liability. Value is far too confusing a term when applied in this way.

We must be more refined in our thinking. Value is not a stable enough term to use in our definition of creativity, or our new understanding.

****

Perhaps the point is best made by the story of Vincent van Gogh. This artist is recognised as a very distinctive, original and creative painter. He lived, worked and died, in the second half of the 19th Century. Many are familiar with his story.

No one valued his work in his lifetime. Few recognised its value until long after his death: not until the context had changed and the story of his tortured life and tragic suicide had been attached to the artworks.

Only then did the value of his art, financial and aesthetic, become apparent. The value of van Gogh's work has varied over its existence, from worthless to priceless. And, in the next five hundred years, it might just become worthless and priceless again, many times over– depending upon the context.

Countless artists, and their works, have suffered these fortunes, along with innumerable scientists, philosophers and inventors. Many have ridden the stormy sea of awe and condemnation. And, of course, many are still waiting to become valuable.

Whatever the merits of Vincent van Gogh's work, we cannot link its creativity to its ambiguous value, or the fickle opinions of critics, commentators, partners, markets and relatives. If we were to use value as an indicator of creativity most of the creative products of humanity would have been assigned to landfill long before the paint had dried or the patent filed.

Some commentators link two or more adjectives together to make a more complex definition of creativity. '*Original and of value*' is often used to define and try to assess creativity. This phrase is used by many educational systems to identify and even define creativity. But this is just a conjunction of two foggy terms combined to create a thicker fog.

Imagine a teacher having to assess creativity in a student's work, when anything the student has not done before is original, and everything they do can have some sort of value.

If the student has never made a pot before, then any pot they make will be original to them. Furthermore, the pot may have immense value to the student–or their mother.

These terms may have some use when discussing and *evaluating* a student's attempt at making things. But they are not precise enough to assess or define creativity. And they certainly do not aid our understanding.

Many adjectives have been applied to creativity. But, once again, the vagueness of these terms is a symptom of the problem – the fuzziness is the proof we do not understand creativity.

We use unclear and imprecise words because our understanding is unclear and imprecise. We use vague and cloudy expressions because our understanding is vague and cloudy.

Creativity, on one level, is very simple, but this simplicity means it presents itself to us in many different ways.

The Inuit vocabulary for snow is fabled to be much larger than that of people from temperate regions. This is because they have an intimate, comprehensive and necessary understanding of their environment.

Similarly, we need to immerse ourselves in the slush and drizzle of creativity to develop a new lexicon.

We need to name, explain, understand and identify the many ways creativity presents itself to us. This lexicon needs to be embedded in our new understanding.

1.6. THE CLASSROOM AND CREATIVITY.

Earlier, I examined the idea that creativity is linked to certain artistic domains. Allied to this idea is the notion that creativity is the preserve of small pockets of our education systems, such as art, drama, dance, music and parts of English.

This institutional and political myopia has wilfully contributed to the idea that some parts of the school curriculum are creative whilst others are not.

Regrettably, this cultural malaise infects our education systems and affects all of us. These ideas have resulted in the misuse and misunderstanding of creativity throughout society.

This traditional view claims the 'uncreative subjects' are more difficult, serious, academic and worthwhile. Allegedly, the uncreative subjects demand more intelligence are more important and have a higher value.

The corollary of this is, the so-called creative subjects are often viewed as little more than a diversionary hobby: something you might engage in if you can't do anything else – subjects that you, *"Do to relax after a hard day with the serious subjects."* [To quote one of my former head teachers.]

Many people believe that 'creative subjects' do not make a serious contribution to society, or embolden a student's education. Some people think that 'creative subjects' are a waste of time, and they are not 'proper education'.

Many educators think of creativity as an indefinable rarity, confined to a few obscure areas of human activity, an unimportant educational oddity – desirable but not essential – and often a little strange. They see 'creative subjects' as an insignificant leisure pursuit, ensconced in the Art Department, on the other side of the playground, kept apart from the 'serious' work of the school.

Naturally, these attitudes extend to parents, the community, teachers – including teachers of 'creative subjects' – universities, the media, politicians and the public. After all, these people have succeeded in this structure; they are products of this system.

In fact, we have all been inculcated with this self-perpetuating nonsense. These primary and very resilient ideas are infused in the bedrock of our education systems. However, a few moments of thought will show the shocking nonsense it scarcely conceals.

****

A long-time complaint of many observers of education is that schools just pump facts and figures into students, then the schools test them to see how much the students remember. This model represents the school as an 'exam factory'.

The other complaint is that schools do not teach enough creativity. Consequently, there has been a long-standing imperative, from many quarters, to teach more of it. They argue that schools need to teach more 'creative art subjects' and the 'exam factories' need to be reformed.

I cannot argue against that prescription. Students certainly need to spend more time on 'creative subjects', and we definitely need to overhaul our schools to balance an inadequate and lop-sided curriculum. But we are wrong if we think by teaching them art-based subjects we are teaching them creativity.

Schools do not teach creativity, and they never have. I repeat, schools do not teach creativity, and they never have.

Creativity cannot be taught because no one really knows what it is. Until now, there has been no cohesive theory of creativity to pass on to students, and there is no acceptable understanding or workable definition of creativity. Consequently, we do not have a culture that understands creativity. Therefore, we cannot teach it. We make the erroneous assumption that art-based subjects and creativity are synonymous. They are not

We think that by teaching students 'creative arts' subjects we are teaching them creativity. We are not.

We may as well teach students how to drive and expect them to be mechanics; or teach them how to sew and expect them to manage a clothes shop. Studying arts subjects and learning about creativity are not the same.

If we want to teach the nature and function of creativity, so that students can understand and direct their creativity, we have to teach it explicitly. And we need to link it with all subjects, not just the art-based ones. As we have seen, creativity affects all domains – and it is part of all school subjects.

There is a vain hope that we can teach creativity by allowing students to play the recorder, write poems and make paper-mâché masks.

Undoubtedly, these sorts of activities can allow aspects of art and craft to flower. These subjects certainly teach a valuable part of human knowledge, and we need to spend more time on them.

But these subjects do not teach students about creativity, and they do not teach them how to be creative. The long-lived idea that by teaching these craft skills we are teaching creativity just confuses the student and everyone else involved in the process.

This attitude misrepresents creativity – reducing it to a mysterious 'non-intellectual' arcane skill or craft. Consequently, some people claim 'creative subjects' are easy, best suited to the 'non-intellectual' and those that are 'best at working with their hands'.

Our schools teach what our societies already know; creativity explores what we do not know. Creativity is the research and development department of humanity; school is its data storage division.

Schools' purpose is to put 'old heads on young shoulders'– test for the efficacy of this process– then grade students according to those tests. The last thing schools want is to encourage students to explore new territories. There is no time for that.

They have to be stuffed – like French geese – with existing knowledge: with things that are already known.

What a start to a creative life this ignorance produces. By the end of their school careers, our children have had their creative blood chased from their veins– to be replaced with the thick, fat, heart-stopping sclerotic cholesterol of 'the system'.

Is it any wonder so many in our communities are suffering mental illnesses, claiming benefits, abusing drugs and are locked away in prisons? Many are still trying to make sense of what they experienced at school. They are still trying to pick apart the mess of conflicting information and cultural values they were taught in the most formative years of their lives.

Most importantly, they are still trying to work out the bits that are missing: the stuff they have not been taught. Such as, an understanding of creativity, and the necessity and importance of being able to examine their unique characters and experiences.

As a culture, we need to see the value of investing money and resources in a vital and meaningful education that makes sense to all those that take part in it.

We need to stop bludgeoning our children and teachers with demands for higher productivity and 'better' results.

Grading students, teachers and schools by their test results is as counterproductive as paying police officers by the number of arrests they make, valuing surgeons for the number of operations they perform, or applauding musicians for the number of songs they can play.

We teach the knowledge of our cultures without explaining how creativity came to make those cultures. Without an understanding of creativity, the time-honoured information – that society is desperately trying to impart– becomes abstract and meaningless.

What is the point of learning old knowledge if we cannot produce new knowledge from it with creativity? Under these principles, education becomes a wheelbarrow without its wheel.

We teach our children how to play the game by copying out the rulebook. Knowledge becomes the self-assembly instructions on an empty box.

Why do we not start with understanding creativity, and then study the results of it? Schools should recognise creativity as part of every subject. It should be taught as part of every child's understanding of the world.

Creativity is the foundation of all knowledge, and it should be a fundamental part of every person's education.

Of course, we have to pass on certain values, knowledge and conventions, but this malformed, half-system of traditional education does not work. It has failed, and continues to fail, generations of children that intuitively reject what is being offered. It fails because we do not recognise the significance of creativity, and we are unable to teach it.

We should bring this structure into the open to inspect its principles – in particular, its indifference to creativity.

If we were to teach our children about creativity, along with its relationship with existing knowledge and the status quo, the traditional curriculum would begin to make sense to many more people. Students would, at last, understand the value and the importance of the information that society tries to pass on to them, and they would appreciate the relationship between an individual's creativity and communal knowledge.

For that to happen, we must know what creativity is. We must be able to understand its architecture, and know how it can be taught.

After decades of involvement with 'creative subjects', it is my observation that creative illiteracy, from all quarters of society, remains our most fundamental problem.

We need to recognize that the exploration and understanding of this universe is a product of Mankind's creative behaviour, not a result of its deference to the status quo.

We need to celebrate the iridescent creative behaviour of all the scientists, mathematicians, entertainers, explorers, artists, entrepreneurs, failures and thinkers, and the billions of ordinary people that have pushed back the borders in our lives.

Most importantly, we need to appreciate that our outmoded educational systems are antithetical to creativity, and they need to be transformed to accommodate this most vital of human behaviours.

1.7. BORN CREATIVE?

There is a very strong traditional view that claims creativity is a rare mystical talent that only a small percentage of people are gifted with before they are born. This long-standing myth suggests that creativity is an entrenched feature of a person's character, and it is applied to all parts of their lives. Under this premise a person is born creative or uncreative.

This idea is rooted in ancient religious beliefs about the nature and origin of the human character.

Of course, these theories are wrong: there is no proof that there is a supernatural force responsible for distributing creativity. And there is no evidence to suggest that some people are born creative while others are not.

However, when people claim that creativity is something we are born with, they are not totally wrong. We are born with creativity, but it is something we are all born with. We all have the ability to be creative; it's just that some do not bother to use the capability. When we choose to use it, some use it at a little, and some use it a lot. We each choose how we use creativity in our lives – and at what level.

But it is important to understand, none of us use creativity all the time. Mostly, we are content to use ordinary, uncreative behaviour to conduct our daily lives, only using creative behaviour when the situation demands it. The bigger the challenge, the higher the level of creativity we use.

Because these creative challenges are often fleeting and short; the creative behaviour is also fleeting and short. We stop behaving creatively when they leave the band, change jobs, complete the research, grow up, solve the equation, or put the last touches to the novel.

In other words, creativity is not a constant force that someone uses all their lives. Creativity is a transient, variable behaviour that we use for short periods of time– when it is needed.

Even during longer bursts of creativity, which might last months –even years, we do not spend all of our days being creative. Every now and then, we have to stop our creative behaviour, and return to ordinary behaviour, so we can maintain our everyday existence.

There has to be time, between the creative high points, for the mundane necessities of life: walking the dog, paying the bills, talking to the children,

During these challenging times, we can observe that creativity is usually confined to a single activity or domain. The novelist will confine their creative behaviour to the book they are writing, the scientist to the experiment they are devising, the dancer to the movements they are choreographing. We do not use creative behaviour in every part of our lives indiscriminately.

From this we can see, there is no such thing as the special person born with creativity– just people that behave creatively some of the time.

In this way, creativity is like many other behaviours. We are all born with the potential to be happy, angry, brave, confident, thoughtful, intelligent, stupid and funny – and we are all born with the ability to be creative. But we cannot always be intensely angry, outrageously funny or blissfully happy, and we cannot use creativity all the time.

This is one of the reasons why creativity has maintained a reputation of being mercurial and mysterious: creativity comes and goes in response to the varying challenges we encounter.

Of course, we cannot expect those that make a living from 'being creative' to dispel these ancient misunderstandings. After all, they have a vested interest in the old-fashioned myths of the mysterious creative person.

It is good press to present yourself as 'a chosen one', in some way superior – perhaps touched by the supernatural at birth– born with special powers; or, at least, affect a coy insouciance and dodge the denial.

This old-fashioned stance does little for the study and understanding of creativity, but it does improve the aura, the fan base, the film rights and tee-shirt sales.

TARQUINS DIARY.

It is just as well that creativity is intermittent and only used when needed. Can you imagine living with someone that is permanently creative? A person that applies creativity to all situations and domains. Life would be impossible.

Tarquin Vesuvius is such a person [an invented character]. Tarquin is not his real name: he changed it when he was twelve years old, then again when he was twenty-two.

Here is an excerpt from his diary. Tarquin wrote it with an aardvark's quill, dipped in ink concocted from blackcurrants and snail excrement. It is written on handmade paper, created from the pulp of reformed bus tickets.

I have translated this excerpt from the unique hieroglyphic language Tarquin composed when he was seven years old.

3:12 a.m. Got out of bed. I made the bed out of rusty sheets of corrugated iron sewn together with barbed wire. I had a wash in vodka and ice cream, then I shaved right leg.

*3:29 a.m. Got dressed in the clothes I have been wearing for the past lunar month. These are all worn inside out, of course. **If this is love – so be it.***

3:46 a.m. Went back to bed and slept under it until the next alarm rings.

8:13 a.m. Had breakfast: today it is tuna milkshake with porridge and hot cherries, drunk from a coffee pot.

8:37 a.m. Into the loft to start work on my current masterwork. I feel very inspired [and a little unwell.]

9:05 a.m. I have sewn a button on the life-size sculpture of myself. The sculpture is made out of old baked bean cans stuffed with mackerel cheesecake. I intend to exhibit the sculpture by setting it alight in the park.

10:32 a.m. Wrote some poetry in Mediaeval Russian about my love for a vacuum cleaner – it sucks.

12:34 p.m. Had another visit from the neighbours. They say I need to stop making beer in the dustbins from bits of lawn and tree bark.

They say, if I do not stop, they will get me evicted. I say [in a French accent], "I do not care as long as I can film the eviction. I shall put it to music and choreograph the event." They seem quite interested in the idea.

1:23 p.m. I rang the Royal Philharmonic Orchestra to see if they were available next month, but they say they are booked up for weeks in advance.

No worry. I shall play all of the instruments myself....

No! I shall make all the instruments, then play them myself.

This is a depiction of just one morning of a person born with the supernatural gift of creativity. Someone unable to control or focus their inborn creativity. A person incarcerated in the lonely, dysfunctional world of the permanently creative.

57

This diary shows that innate creativity, applied to all domains, all the time, would be a burden– not a gift.

In our new understanding, we have to acknowledge that creativity is not something gifted from a supernatural authority; it is a behaviour we all possess.

Creativity is a variable and intermittent behaviour that we can all draw upon to improve our lives – if we understand how it works.

1.8. BORN UNCREATIVE?

On the other side of this idea – just as popular – is the notion that creativity is an attribute that can go missing at birth. This is the same ancient misunderstanding applied differently.

Often, outwardly intelligent people will revel in the idea they were born uncreative. Arms crossed, they announce – to all that will listen– they are not creative. They wear the 'I am not creative' badge like a piece of armour, with pride, and point to it regularly for protection. The self-proclaimed 'uncreative person' builds an impenetrable prison, starting at the bars of the cot. They are encouraged by teachers and parents – who venerate being right and 'good'.

They reject being wrong, stupidity, messing about, experimentation and play. These granite walls of conformity become conceptual dungeons where they behave themselves. These old ideas, that cause some people to reject creative behaviour, expose a popular underlying aversion. For many, the claim that they were born uncreative wards off any association with the negative connotations of creativity. These people dig a deep foxhole in the safe, sensible and logical world of the status quo. They run scared of the perceived – and real – irrationality, danger and general 'fluffiness' of creativity.

As we have seen, creativity can be a difficult behaviour to live with, especially when used at a high-level; consequently, for many, it is easier to claim genetic or spiritual paucity.

Rejecting the idea that they are born creative avoids the risks involved in this behaviour, which could upset carefully ordered lives. We live in a world where being correct – all the time, in all situations – is a highly prized attribute. We invest an enormous amount of time and energy in striving to do things 'properly' and getting things 'right'. We rejoice in passing the test, in appearing to be clever and having everything under control.

By claiming to have missed the mythical creativity gene, or being spiritually unlucky, the self-proclaimed 'uncreatives' do not have to deal with the embarrassment and emotional anguish of getting it wrong or appearing foolish, that often accompanies creative behaviour. For many people, life is easier, less complicated and safer without creativity.

SOCIETY SUPPORTS THE STATUS QUO.

Why are so many people happy to consider themselves to be uncreative? Why do we accept the rejection of such an important part of human character?

I think it is more than the fact that creativity is a risky behaviour or because we are inclined to reject failure. Undoubtedly, these leanings are a part of the equation, but these characteristics are also a symptom of a much deeper human condition.

Society is, by nature, conservative.

All societies are naturally biased towards supporting the safety of the status quo and rejecting the potential risks and hazards that accompany creativity and change.

Creativity is a natural human behaviour that has the power to change the world. This means it is a scary proposition to those that enjoy the safety, security and benefits of the world as it is. If you are someone in the echelon of power, creativity is something that needs to be controlled and moderated. Encouraging the population to celebrate their natural creativity might lead to all sorts of difficult situations.

I think these naturally occurring sentiments have influenced the way society manages creativity. I think there is a natural fear of creativity which produces a tendency for schools and parents to moderate and dampen our children's creativity.

Perhaps unwittingly. Maybe with intent. More likely something in between.

This inclination involves discouraging or suppressing behaviour that is seen as different, abnormal or that questions the way things are done.

Part of the function of schools is to act as agents, promotors and protectors of tradition and the status quo. The teaching and learning contract is dependent on the idea that the older and wiser adult will mould, inform and shape the young student into a version of themselves. This individual contract is magnified in the behaviour of societal leaders and the common people.

The leaders of society have spent a long history organising everything to their liking. They do not want to hand over the ability to make perilous changes to those that do not share the leaders' values.

Under this understanding our status quo is the best version of the totality of ourselves.

This battle between the conservative pressures of the community and the unpredictable natural creativity of the individual, often causes problems when mishandled or misunderstood: intuitive creativity and individuality can become stifled.

But creativity and individuals are indomitable, they rise in all sorts of ways, and in all sorts of diverse behaviours. Many of these behaviours are abhorrent to those intent on maintaining the status quo, and those interested in controlling and managing society.

Unfortunately, we are rarely aware of this 'socialisation' process. We are not invited to discuss, explore or examine these influences on our lives. This is the reality we are issued at birth.

For this reason, we are led to deny our individual creativity, and learn how to behave as normal, 'satisfactory' people: we fold our arms and adopt the badge of the uncreative. We are encouraged to make excuses about being born without creative ability. This is the collective value system society inculcates from an early age.

It defines what is a successful student and what is an unsuccessful student. It defines what is a successful school and what is an unsuccessful school.

It is this process of enforced socialisation, that is antithetical to individualism, and the natural creativity we are all born with.

It may seem that I am being critical of the status quo; this is not my intention. We all need to have some sort of social structure in our lives. Whatever shape that takes is defined as the status quo.

I am trying to explain and describe our current situation and examine how it diminishes the natural creativity of millions of people by allowing ancient, misleading and erroneous ideas to continue. I am interested in uncovering these hidden influences so that we can understand them, become aware of them, and are able to deal with them honestly.

If we really want to embrace and understand creativity, we need to come to terms with the natural socialising aspects of parenting, education and the state. We need to explore and understand how, and why, individuality and creativity is discouraged. Finally, we need to change our education systems to accommodate these new understandings, so we can teach and develop everyone's creativity, rather than hide behind ancient ideas that provide excuses for its suppression and removal.

COMMUNAL ADVANTAGE OF CREATIVITY.

We have rejected the idea that creativity is some sort of supernatural interference in rare babies, before birth.

But there is another more modern idea linking creativity with birth that is worth considering. This idea claims that creativity is passed to the unsuspecting baby through their genes. This leads to the common claim that a person is not creative because they missed the creativity gene.

This idea is worth considering– but not for long.

As we have seen, we are all born with the ability to be creative. And we are all born with a unique but similar genetic heritage, honed by our species over billions of years of evolution to help us survive.

We can imagine that slight variations in our genes could affect our behaviours, causing some people to be more confident to take on the challenges of creative behaviour than others.

We might also assume that confidence with creative behaviour may be advantageous to the individual and increase their chances of surviving into adulthood to reproduce creative offspring. In other words, there may be a link between genes and creativity.

But this idea does not stand close observation.

To have a selective advantage, creativity genes would have to provide a benefit to the individual; that benefit would then have to improve their chances of producing children with a similar aptitude for creativity.

However, creativity rarely provides that benefit. Although creativity may cause some to enjoy a better life than some, we have seen from Tarquin's diary that creativity can also be a burden. Often, in the extreme, creativity can terminate lives prematurely, and stop the passage of genes.

The enquiring creative nature can cause someone to wander too close to 'the edge' and not return. In which case, any genetic advantage would be abruptly cancelled.

People that behave with creativity often ask troublesome and dangerous questions: What will happen if I prod the sleeping bear with this stick? I wonder what this mushroom tastes like? If I stand on the cliff and wave my arms like a bird, will I be able to fly?

Sometimes the results of creative behaviour can stop gene transfer alarmingly quickly. Many inquisitive minds have been sacrificed on the altar of creativity. For this reason, it is difficult to find a selective advantage for all the individuals that use creative behaviour.

However, we can imagine there is a big selective advantage in conforming with the 'normal' behaviour of the community. Conforming and obeying the accrued wisdom that forms the status quo – doing what the rest of the community does – is the surest and safest way to pass on genes. If anything provides a selective advantage it is conformity.

That, of course, is why we teach it to our children.

But we must not dismiss the evolutionary impact of creativity too lightly. We can imagine that there is a profound selective advantage to the **community** [and species] that has members that behave creatively.

The surviving community learns about bears, mushrooms and flying in a most memorable fashion.

In which case, individual creativity can definitely improve the selective advantage of a **community** that are party to an individual's creativity.

Creativity, like all behaviour, is the result of a hotchpotch of disparate genes and mutable behaviours, that are challenged by fluctuating environments and beliefs.

Genes may be part of that equation, but they do not necessarily convey evolutionary success to the individual. However, creativity is essential to the survival and evolution of the community– and the species.

It is time we stopped excusing ourselves from embracing and understanding creative behaviour, by blaming lost genes or wayward spirits.

We need to forge a better understanding of creativity, and learn how to teach and nurture the ability to be creative in all of our children.

1.9. CREATIVITY FOR THE WEIRD.

Many people think of creativity as the behaviour of 'weird' people. The idea that creativity happens outside of regular behaviour is very strong. Because of this connection with strangeness, creativity has for a long time been connected with the eccentric, the odd and the maladjusted; consequently, it often attracts the eccentric, the odd and the maladjusted.

Sometimes they are also creative – sometimes not. Often, the creative people are the temperate ones, sitting at the back, in the dark suits. But it is easy to become deceived into thinking that because someone looks 'different' they are creative; however, 'strange' physical appearances and odd behaviours are not a defining characteristic of creativity or creative people.

Dressing 'funny' and doing strange things to your hair will not make you more creative, and being creative will not turn your hair blue. There is no such thing as a creative person, just people that behave creatively... sometimes. Sometimes they employ 'funny' fashion; sometimes they do not. Creativity cannot be defined by someone's choice of clothes, haircut or lifestyle.

****

Some people think of creativity as being linked to madness. Circumstantial evidence of this connection comes in countless stories about 'creative' people that have behaved a little oddly: Caravaggio Stubbs, van Gogh, Mozart, Plath, Bosch, Munch, Wolfe, Hemmingway, Schumann.

The list is extensive; each had a strange story to tell. But for every headline eccentric, there are innumerable stable, ordinary people behaving creatively in the middle pages. These people have less scandalous, and less memorable, tales to tell.

Yes, you have to think and behave differently to be creative. Creative behaviour is certainly different from 'normal' behaviour, but you can't act with creativity all of the time, and you do not have to have mental health issues, or be criminally insane, to think and behave differently.

This idea would have more value if all people with a mental illness engaged in creative behaviour, and if all people that have engaged in creative behaviour could be shown to suffer a psychosis. Consequently, being a little 'weird' is not a good enough quality to be used in our new understanding, or our new definition.

However, it does make sense that creativity is associated with alternative thinking. So that begs the question: does creativity attract alternative thinkers, or does alternative thinking make you a little abnormal?

But just as politics draws the bossy, accountancy draws the numerate, modelling draws the gaunt and acting draws the show-offs, those activities that have traditionally been associated with creativity often attract the outsiders of the community. Either because they are behaving differently, or because they want to be seen as different. Neither characteristic guarantees creativity.

Sometimes 'weirdness' is an expression of wanting to think and behave differently. Strange behaviour can be seen as a dissatisfaction with the status quo. But dissatisfaction is not enough. It is a good starting point, but you have to do something about changing the status quo if you are going to be creative.

Many inhabit the so-called creative domains as a sanctuary from the real world. They claim the cloudy protection of the 'creative environment' so they do not have to justify their existence to a world that does not understand the 'creative temperament'. In short, creativity – particularly in the artistic domains – is often used as an excuse for not wishing to be accountable, objective or conventional–for behaving a bit 'weird'. The explanation 'they are just creative' becomes a satin-lined cloak for the eccentric, the peculiar and the dissolute to hide behind.

Here we have a simple fact that reinforces an earlier observation: many people are wary, even afraid, of creativity and the people that display creative behaviour. Because creativity has, so far, been ill-defined, and surrounded by this soft-focus woolliness, it opens the door to all sorts of dubious characters asserting their 'creativity'. In the misty world of creativity, the language of '*Je ne sais quoi*' is paramount: it is writ large in notes for exhibition catalogues, artist's statements or the appraisal of the sycophantic critic. Claims of spirituality, esoteric feelings, subjective notions, magical qualities, atmosphere, otherness, mysticism and fascinations with the obscure are golden coinage in the realm of the creative.

These creative contenders should not be criticised too harshly for this: the desire to be creative, to entertain, make new things, just be a 'hanger-on' or spectate from the wings, is often the precursor for great things.

But then so is the insensitive criticism of an intolerant and belligerent community. Consequently, for many, the realms of creativity are bursting with distrust. Is she a genius? Is she a fraud? Perhaps both.

Because people that behave with creativity are sometimes seen as being a bit weird, crazy, wayward and unpredictable, they scare those that consider themselves uncreative – and all those that anchor themselves to 'normal' behaviour.

The self-claimed 'uncreatives' hunker down in their uncrazy, sober, reliable, safe bunkers – only peering out when all those funny, weird, creative people have thundered past.

But of course, their instincts are right.

If the creativity produced by these people has any value, it is because it is suffused with the power to change our lives, to wrestle us from our sobriety, to release us from our good manners and civilisation – from our solid, safe status quo.

Creativity has the power to shake the footings of all we hold dear: to solve the problem of our steadfast normality.

LIZARDS

Creativity can make us dance like poisoned lizards,

scream like broken bells, rant like drunken priests.

We all know it because it frightens us –

sometimes a little, sometimes a lot.

In that fear, it excites us.

It makes our minds tingle and burn.

It picks the rusty locks, and it tears down the dusty drapes.

It makes us laugh; it makes us fume.

It makes us feel alive – so we crave it.

It is a chemical. It sneaks through our senses.

It transforms our lives.

It corrupts us, addicts us, distorts us, warps us.

It evolves us,

and then it leaves us:

just a little more strange

than we were at breakfast.

kjb.

1.10. HARD WORK MAKES YOU CREATIVE.

There is a very popular idea that claims you have to spend many years in study, toil and application before you are able to be successful in a 'creative' domain.

This is not very incisive advice.

We must assume that if you were to play snooker every evening for three years, you would get better at it, and if you studied the violin eight hours a day, you would be a better musician after five years than after two weeks.

It makes sense that if you engaged with any activity for ten years you would improve your performance over time, and you would be more successful at the end of the time than at the beginning.

The hard work argument is hardly a revelation.

But the idea creativity can only happen *after* you have spent enormous amounts of time involved in an activity, and hard work is the pathway to creativity and success, and you will not be creative or successful before these 'dues' have been paid, is frivolous.

This idea reduces creativity and success to an apprenticeship, or a series of routine tasks that have to be completed, over a long period of time, before creativity and success can occur.

If only it were as simple as this!

Unfortunately, there are tens of thousands of unsuccessful artists, inventors, business people, dancers, scientists and writers that have spent far more than ten years pursuing their dreams, but they are no closer to creativity or success than the day they started. Success and creativity are oleaginous and capricious friends: we cannot guarantee their acquaintance, or loyalty, simply by working long and hard.

And for all those that have spent back-curving, face-lining decades struggling to be creative and successful in their chosen domain, how about all of those annoying people that were successful without even trying?

There are many examples, but the story of Orson Welles and his seminal film, '*Citizen Kane',* is a wonderful example – familiar to many. As a twenty-seven-year-old novice film-maker, Orson Welles co-wrote, produced, directed and starred in one of the most creative, successful and influential films ever made.

The essence of this story is repeated many thousands of times over, with debut novels, one-hit wonders, opening nights at the theatre, inventions on the back of envelopes, scientific experiments that have – by accident or coincidence – produced creative products of phenomenal importance.

This is creative success invoked in a nanosecond. Long before the curtains have opened, or the audience has reached their seats. Let alone decades of drudgery in a cold garret, basement lab or rehearsal room, pandering to a Victorian work ethic.

And what of those people who have completed their decades of apprenticeship in a domain?

Perhaps in their youth they had the elation of being recognised as a successful creative person only to fail miserably in their cold-toed dotage.

Surely, once these 'successful creatives' had served their ten years of apprenticeship they could live out the rest of their lives in the comfortable knowledge they had succeeded in obtaining their 'creativity credentials'. But the roll-call of once creative 'greats' that have died in unsuccessful, uncreative and dismal poverty is measured in light-years.

What happened?

How did creativity abandon them? Even after they had done all the hard work, achieved success and passed their decades of training?

It does not make sense.

It appears creativity can take years to surface – yet it can be gone in a flash. It can also fail after fifty years of success, then happen, as if by magic, to a five-year-old.

The question for us is... Why? Why should creativity blow up, then puff and stall, only to pop up again to flop once more?

What are the greasy structures that underpin this most slippery of behaviours?

Certainly, the people trying to be creative and successful are not lacking in time and effort.

Although, I do not doubt diligence and industry can help creativity – it is no guarantee of it.

If this were the case, the most creative and the most successful people would be the oldest, most experienced and the hardest working.

There is no relation between the amount of time and effort applied to creative activities and success.

We cannot define creativity or success as something that is the result of years of hard work. Consequently, we cannot use this idea as a basis for our new understanding.

1.11. THE CREATIVITY OF GODS.

This is probably the most common, and oldest, idea about creativity: creativity as a phenomenon that emanates from a supernatural authority. This idea proposes that creative behaviour has something to do with gods and religion. This interpretation of creativity is a legacy from long ago: a time when our ancestor's lives were dominated and controlled by a religious doctrine–of one sort or another.

Around the world, religious dogma still influences large portions of community life, including our political and state structures, medical practices, criminal justice systems and educational philosophies. The trenchant nature of these religious traditions is understandable: if your culture has been immersed in religion since its beginning, it would be very difficult to cast aside these ancient beliefs, and their attendant social practices, without experiencing some damp residue.

Today, many areas of life are drying out and minimising the effects of religion, replacing it with a more modern, secular and enlightened view. Except, of course, in our understanding of creativity.

For many people, creativity is still explained as a supernatural energy, driven by the mystical influences of gods. As we saw earlier, some people believe creativity is something only special 'god-touched' people are born with. If you believe in a religion this will probably be your prevailing view.

There are very good reasons for this connection between creativity and the supernatural. Creativity is a behaviour that displays many properties that appear to have an air of the supernatural about them. Creativity operates outside of the dull spheres of 'normal' human behaviour. Creativity provides thoughts and products that sometimes appear–without reason–from an unknown and therefore mystical place. Creativity can appear to summon ideas and behaviours from 'nowhere', to improve the quality of our lives – and enthral us.

Even secular-inclined people find it difficult to describe where their creativity comes from. Often, we are told their creative ideas mysteriously 'pop' into their heads, as if by magic.

With such a profile, viewed through the fine mesh of thousands of years of religious doctrine, it is not surprising many people find creativity to be an enigmatic and mystical attribute, which is most easily explained as coming from somewhere 'otherworldly'.

This situation is made worse by science and secular thought not having a plausible explanation. Consequently, the way is open for religions, and the religious, to continue with their claims. [Until now.]

This long-standing link with religion and the divine, accounts for the outmoded spiritual and paranormal associations of creativity. It also explains why those that behave with high level creativity, have often, over the centuries, attained a highly revered social status – along with the domains they labour in.

Because, in the past, the architecture of creativity has been muddled and difficult to understand, we have allowed this dense thicket of ideas, beliefs and conventions, to grow more impenetrable.

If you have a religious conviction, you do not need me to clarify where creativity comes from, or define it for you. In which case, this book can stand as a primer, explaining the way that gods have influenced humanity to use creativity.

However, if you do not believe in a god – if you do not have a religion, or you are not sure – you may like to examine the underlying structure of creativity, and consider how it can be defined. You will reject the idea – as I do – that a definition that includes references to gods, religion, magic or the supernatural is acceptable. We need a more worldly, more modern, explanation.

Whatever your belief, to continue to leave creativity unexplored and fog-bound [or even god-bound]; conceived of as a mysterious phenomenon, unknowable by Mankind, is an indefensible situation.

The understanding of creativity is too important a subject to leave to gods.

We need to waft away the incense, open the windows, and reveal the mundane workings of creativity.

As with all good tricks, once we know how it is done the mystery dissolves.

1.12. INSPIRATION.

As we have seen, many people accept the idea that creativity has some sort of supernatural dimension, which they associate with religious beliefs. However, some hold a slightly different conception of the spiritual link. These people think we all have the 'creative spirit' deep inside us. They believe we just have to find the right stimulus to unleash this peculiar force, revealing the path to a 'higher plane', enabling a communication with a greater being, or an unknown creative energy.

This idea posits creativity as part of the human psyche, a hidden part of our character, 'spirit' or 'soul', that can only be accessed by imbibing certain foods and drink.

This is a very ancient and popular idea. These foods, drinks and behaviours – these joggers of the creative constitution – are supposed to 'inspire' people that want to be creative.

These mental obstruction removers, have often been consumed, or invoked, when there is creative work to be done, a problem is to be solved – or when a closer connection with an imagined supernatural force is desired.

But if all that was needed to be creative was a bottle of cider or a puff on a joint, any city centre pub or bar on a Saturday night would be awash with revellers, writing operas in Cantonese, designing perpetual motion engines from bottle tops, and experimenting with new recipes for chocolate-dipped coconut and cherry shortbread. Unfortunately, this is not the case.

People that would like to be creative, consume this sort of thing for the same reason that anybody else does: they want to party.

It is, of course, a lovely notion: just take the creativity pill, creativity drink, or creativity smoke, and you will unleash all of your suppressed creative potential.

This idea is still popular with many seekers of creativity, people who wish to see the world in a new light – those that want to gain access to a more truthful vision – those that want to get closer to some form of god; however, if we are honest...it's just an excuse to get giddy and dance till comatose.

If you are searching for inspiration, the chosen 'medicine' may unshackle your talents. But more often, what we find is a release from the constraints of our normality and the restrictions of our status quo. Sometimes partying can result in creativity, sometimes not.

There is no doubt many famous names have claimed certain 'additives' have improved their creativity. Unfortunately, there is also very sharp-edged and hard evidence that these 'creativity condiments' have shortened many thousands of lives before they managed to produce a title, prime a canvas or tune their instruments.

Furthermore, some have found these additives have made their, once focused, creative minds a little fuzzy around the edges.

Beware: partying can be a dangerous business – *if you do it properly.*

The alcoholic writer, the drug-addicted performer, the spliff smoking musician, the self-administering scientist; all are seared into the popular consciousness. Along with many others that relied on the idea that creativity can be found, released or inspired, by an imbibed chemical or other substances.

For myself, whenever I have thought my dancing, singing, conversation or ideas to save the world, were being improved by external stimuli, more sober people usually tell me otherwise.

The rule, of course, is... avoid partying with the abstemious, and never dance with the sober.

I have found – after extensive research – a prompt start without interruption is the best tonic for creativity. The truth is, we do not *need* external additives to be creative. Creativity is not dependent on shamanic concoctions, hangovers, or Sunday mornings in the cells.

It is, however, aided by an understanding of the architecture of creativity and the application of rigorous thought processes. Once these procedures are complete, what better way to celebrate than to roll back the carpet and have a party?

****

There are other well-established ideas about inspiration, that do not require a shrivelling of the brain or a desecration of the liver. A common idea claims that if you keep your mind open and are receptive, or you place yourself in a sympathetic environment, you may just be able to gain motivation from some beautiful being or interesting object.

This sort of inspiration is the simplest and softest expression of the external stimulant.

The thinking goes like this: if you wait for long enough, and you keep your senses primed, and you focus on the required problem, eventually you will be **inspired** to be creative.

Waiting for inspiration appears to be the complement to the idea that you have to **work hard** before you can be creative. In this version of the idea you have to **wait hard**. This notion has been around for thousands of years.

Once again, we can find a link with gods and the supernatural. This time the idea goes right back to the birth of civilisation. The Ancient Greeks believed in *'The Daughters of Zeus'*. These were a collection of nine gods of creativity. The Greeks called them Muses; each one was responsible for a particular 'creative domain'.

Along with many other Ancient Greek ideas, this concept still influences our lives today. Muse is a root for a number of modern words linked with creativity: music, museum, musing, amusing, bemused.

The Ancient Greeks believed Muses would make contact from the heavens and empower a chosen earthly mortal to produce creative works.

It was thought that a Muse had the power to breathe creativity into an ordinary person: literally, to 'inspire' the heavenly spirit into the mind and body of a mortal maker.

The artist, or creative person, was conceived of as a sort of earth-bound receiver for the godly qualities of the Muse: a direct connection between heaven and earth – the mortal and the immortal

In this way, creativity was seen as a divine communication from 'the gods': as a heavenly gift from a supernatural being. Creativity as a 'gift' from the gods is still referenced in our description of *gifted* people. But it was important that the receiver of the Muse's gift was in the correct frame of mind, and ready to accept the inspiration. If the mortal was not receptive – mind cleared of all commonplace, earthly clutter – the Muse might not make a good connection, and the link may not be made. An excellent excuse for writer's block.

This is another reason for some of our present-day mystical misconceptions about inspiration, and the root of our ideas about the whimsical, fickle and magical nature of creativity.

As one of the oldest ideas about creativity, this one carries a lot of cultural weight. There is no doubt, getting yourself organised, clearing a space and focusing on your chosen task is all very good preparation for anyone considering being creative. But the idea you have to stare off into the distance for hours, waiting for divine inspiration from a 'heavenly being', before any creativity can work is indefensible in the twenty-first century.

Therefore, this very ancient and pervasive notion cannot be allowed to continue in our new, post-enlightenment understanding of creativity, or our new definition.

PART TWO

THE IGNORED PARTS OF
CREATIVITY.

After exploring some of the common ideas about creativity, we can see it is a wide-ranging and deeply misunderstood phenomenon. In the past, we have developed many different explanations and definitions in an effort to understand this vital part of Mankind's character. Several of them have become deeply located in the public consciousness.

But when reviewing these traditional viewpoints, there is one jarring fact that sticks out: our existing ideas are unsophisticated and severely limited.

Over the centuries we have pruned and cultivated a notion of creativity that fits in with the prevailing political, religious, educational and social requirements. In this way, we have managed to disregard less agreeable, unwanted areas of creativity that are difficult to accommodate and explain, or that do not fit into the required view or definition.

But these overlooked aspects are essential to our understanding of creativity. The next section identifies and explores some of these vital, but ignored, expressions of creativity.

2.1. LOW-INTENSITY CREATIVE BEHAVIOUR.

One of the most fundamental and ignored facts about creativity is that it is composed of two parts: creative behaviour and the creative product.

For example, we can identify the creative **behaviour** that organises and points the camera, and we can identify the creative **product** of the finished photograph.

These two articles, creative behaviour and the creative product, comprise the amalgam of creativity.

These two parts are very different entities with very different functions and influences.

By examining these parts separately, we are able to open up a much broader view of creativity, and construct a much more cohesive understanding.

Let's start with creative behaviour.

The first thing we notice when considering creative behaviour is that it is not all the same.

When we look closely, and consider it carefully, we can see that there is a wide expression of creative behaviour.

Traditionally, creative behaviour is seen as something that only exists at a very high and rare level.

Some even characterise creativity as the highest achievement of human behaviour.

89

For example, we can imagine a composer might engage in concentrated, and long-lasting, creative behaviour by devoting a lot of time and effort working on a ground-breaking opera or symphony.

This is a traditional notion of creative behaviour.

But it does not take too much thought or observation to realise that creative behaviour does not always entail enormous levels of time, concentration and energy.

For example, less intense creative behaviour might involve someone spending just a few minutes writing a new lyric to the tune of '*Happy Birthday*' for an impromptu birthday celebration.

With the realisation that creative behaviour can vary in its intensity, we can propose a full spectrum of creative behaviour.

THE INTENSITY SPECTRUM OF CREATIVE BEHAVIOUR

LOW-INTENSITY-- HIGH-INTENSITY

Uses little time and effort   Uses lots of time and effort

Generally Ignored   Generally Recognised

At one end of the spectrum, we have high-intensity creative behaviour, and at the other end we can have low-intensity creative behaviour.

And it makes sense that we can have all of the grades between the two extremes: medium-intensity, low-to-medium intensity and medium-to-high intensity creative behaviours.

Traditionally, high-intensity creative behaviour has been easily recognised. However, low-intensity creative behaviour is more difficult to identify and appreciate.

Often, low-intensity creative behaviour operates without any effort: the spontaneous witty comment, the idea that seemingly pops into the head without exertion, the intuitive action.

From this observation, we can see that creativity occupies many more areas of our lives than traditional ideas about creativity might suggest.

Creative behaviour is not just the intense and rare activities of the 'gifted' genius; it is also a common behaviour that many people use and engage with on a daily basis.

****

The recognition of low-intensity creative behaviour, allows us to identify and focus on some interesting features of creativity that in the past have been undervalued or unrecognised.

But that is for later.

First, we must explore the other part of the creativity amalgam: the creative product.

2.2. THE BENEFIT SPECTRUM OF THE CREATIVE PRODUCT.

Just as we can produce a spectrum of creative behaviour, we can also produce a spectrum of the creative product. This spectrum is based on the number of people that find the creative product beneficial.

In the past, when thinking about and describing creative products, we have tended to focus on the results of extraordinary human achievement. This is the stuff we all marvel at: The Sistine Chapel, the exploration of space, the clarinet, the printing press, Baroque music, lemon drizzle cake, Algebra. These are the summits of our creativity country.

These creative products are appreciated by many people; consequently, they occupy the extreme right of the benefit spectrum of the creative product.

However, although these high-benefit creative products are of enormous significance, and represent our traditional understanding of creativity, it makes sense that they are not the only expression of the creative product.

There is no doubt that some creative products benefit a smaller number of people. These creative products are not so easy to identify, and they need to be located further down the spectrum.

Here we can recognise the medium-benefit, low-to-medium benefit and medium-to-high benefit creative products.

And it makes sense that, in the extreme, we can find the creative product that only benefits, or is appreciated, by one person. Usually, this is the person that created the product.

THE BENEFIT SPECTRUM OF THE CREATIVE PRODUCT	
LOW-BENEFIT CREATIVE PRODUCT	HIGH-BENEFIT CREATIVE PRODUCT
One person benefits	Lots of people benefit
Common	Rare
Ignored by all	Applauded by all

Although some creative products do not benefit lots of people, they can often be the result of impassioned people with serious creative intent.

These creative products are undoubtedly the result of high-intensity creative behaviour. However, in the past, we have tended to ignore or undervalue these less-appreciated creative products.

These low-benefit creative products include the painting no one enjoys, the unheard song, the unread novel, the ignored invention, the business that does not make a profit– and my favourite: the misunderstood joke.

For every high-benefit creative product there are millions of unnoticed low-benefit and mid-ground creative products. Consequently, we must admit that the creative product is a much more ubiquitous and commonplace entity than is commonly acknowledged.

Because low-benefit creative products only benefit a small number of people, their makers are often considered to be unsuccessful in their creative labours.

There appears to be a presumption that the low-benefit creative products are deficient in creative behaviour, because only a small number of people appreciate them.

For this reason, we often ignore or undervalue low-benefit creative products, even though the creative behaviour that produced them may have been of very high-intensity.

This is a long-standing error that obscures some important observations about the nature of creativity that we need to explore and understand.

2.3. THE SHIFTING BENEFIT SPECTRUM OF THE CREATIVE PRODUCT.

The establishment of the benefit spectrum reveals a very important characteristic of the creative product that in the past we have ignored.

The position of the creative product on the benefit spectrum is not fixed; the creative product can shift on the benefit spectrum in response to its changing value.

For example, if the low-benefit product, whether it be a painting, song, novel, invention or idea, somehow acquires the appreciation of others, it can become a high-benefit, and very influential, creative product.

This shift in appreciation of the low-benefit creative product can happen in just a few days, but it can also take decades, even centuries.

This observation means we need to view all low-benefit creative products as something of enormous potential and immense importance to our new understanding of creativity.

Not least, because we can see that all creative products start their existence as extreme low-benefit creative products.

For this reason, we can consider the low-benefit creative product as the 'seed' of all creative products, each with the potential to grow into a world-changing high-benefit creative product.

There is a further important observation to be made: the benefit shift of the creative product can happen in the opposite direction.

Frequently, the once essential high-benefit creative product slips down the benefit spectrum, as the number of people that find the creative product beneficial diminishes.

Here lies the once glorious inventions of the stagecoach, the bow and arrow, the telegram, 78 rpm records, platform shoes and much popular music.

From this, we can see that all creative products are destined to constantly shift up and down the benefits spectrum, in response to changing values and prevailing circumstances.

However, for our new understanding of creativity, the most important characteristic of the low-benefit creative product is that it is usually ignored– along with the creative behaviour that produced it.

Traditionally, only when the low-benefit creative product has acquired recognition and has been transformed into a high-benefit creative product, does the creative behaviour involved in its production become appreciated or recognised.

2.4. THE SMALL CREATIVE PRODUCT.

Consider the huge number of domains, skills and knowledge that comprise a big budget movie, a cruise ship, or an ambitious civil engineering development.

Often people will describe these huge undertakings as being creative or uncreative. But this is not very perceptive.

Some large ventures may be entirely creative, but it is rare to be able to describe all parts of a difficult and complex project in such simple, all-encompassing terms.

Often, creativity can be identified in just a small portion of the mostly uncreative theory, performance, equation, recipe or design. When we spot these flashes of creativity in a big, largely uncreative, composition we are witnessing small creativity.

The novel may have a very inventive storyline, but the characters may be conventional. The film may be directed with high-intensity creative behaviour, but the costumes may be tired and dull. The roof of the building may be state-of-the-art, but the rest of the building may be very traditional.

The reasons for this disparity are clear: often, discrete aspects of the composite creative product are created by different people, or teams of people, with different motivations.

Consequently, a multi-faceted product can vary in the creative quality of its components.

But small creativity is not only found in large, complicated projects. Smaller creative products that have been produced by an individual, or a small collection of people, can be deconstructed into constituent parts. These parts may vary in the intensity of their creativity.

In these products, the makers might rely on tried and tested conventions for some areas but they are inspired to use creative behaviour for other parts.

Small creativity is often ignored or missed as it is integrated and swamped by the larger composition.

We need to make sure we recognise small creativity when analysing, evaluating and assessing creative products.

And we need to include small creativity in our new understanding and our new vocabulary.

2.5. MALCREATIVITY.

A consistently ignored aspect of creativity is the creative behaviour used to fashion 'unpleasant' creative products.

Traditionally, we do not recognise the creativity that results in 'bad' creative products, but this is an essential, and unfortunately extremely large, component of Mankind's culture.

So repugnant is the idea creativity can service our most base thoughts and darkest imaginings, we prefer not to admit to its existence. Consequently, 'bad' creativity remains uncharted territory.

As we have seen, many people think of creative behaviour as the apotheosis of human activity and high-benefit creative products as the highest order of human achievement. Consequently, the idea has been promoted that, if we want our lives to be better, all we have to do is be a little more creative.

Creativity has always been presented as a behaviour that only well-intentioned, good people use. If we could just inject ourselves with more creativity, as if we were participants in some futuristic fantasy, the world would be a much more agreeable place. We could waft around in white kaftans reciting poetry, painting bucolic scenes, whilst sipping sweet wine and being excessively polite to each other.

It would be...well... heavenly.

In some people's eyes, creativity always makes for a better world.

But this is arrant nonsense. This conception of creativity is a saccharin dream.

We live in a malignant and magnificent world, formed by humanity's creativity, which is driven by the individual's desire to make their lives better.

Unfortunately, the focus of an individual's creativity is not always on making the world a better place for everyone. Often, a person's creative behaviour is turned against other people, and other species, to fabricate all sorts of unpleasant creative products.

Creativity has led to some wonderful benefits for individuals and their communities. But it has also inspired behaviour and products that are abhorrent, detrimental and repugnant to those that do not belong to that community.

This is the ugly face of creativity: the dark side of our imaginations and behaviours – the use of creativity to subjugate, destroy and behave badly towards others.

This is Malcreativity: creativity that results in nasty deeds and horrific products.

Some of humanity's most monstrous crimes are the result of immense creativity – but we refuse to recognise a connection. In our collective minds, we only apply creativity to the good and the gracious. However, if we take a closer look, we can see there is just as much creative behaviour in the building of an interrogation centre or concentration camp, as there is in the building of a school, museum or hospital.

The torture chamber is full of creative products– designed to inflict pain and fear. The creation of weapons, intended to blow people apart, employs just as much creativity as the tools used in an operating theatre to put them back together.

Creativity is not always warm, soft and life-enhancing for everyone. Creativity does not always result in good things that we all find acceptable. Creativity is not a preserve of the good and the worthy.

Our prisons are brimming with people that have acted with creativity: stealing, defrauding, lying and cheating, killing and maiming – working against, and preying upon, their fellow human beings – using all levels of creative behaviour to further their individual desires.

We can imagine there are even more people outside of prisons – just as distasteful – that have evaded capture... by using their creativity.

The identification of malcreativity opens a large can of worms steeped in oil. How can we forge weapons of torture with the same creativity we use to make tools for surgery? How do we decide what is good creativity and what is bad creativity? How do we define Malcreativity?

Who should make these decisions?

How does Malcreativity sometimes become good creativity?

Why have we always connected creativity with goodness?

Why have we always ignored the bad side of creativity?

Good and bad are subjective values. Just as the value of a creative product can be altered by changing external factors, so the perceived goodness or badness of a creative product is subject to external influences.

Whether the bomb dropped on Hiroshima in 1945 was good or bad depends upon your perspective. Undoubtedly, it was made using high-intensity creative behaviour. But was the bomb an example of good creativity or bad creativity?

Here we can find another spectrum to apply to creativity: The Moral Spectrum.

Theoretically, we can locate each creative product on this spectrum to reflect its moral standing. One end will represent creative products everyone thinks are morally bad: the other end will represent the creative products everyone thinks are morally good. Once again, we can imagine there is an enormous grey area between these extremes.

But perhaps the most important thing about this moral spectrum is the observation that there is no connection between creativity and 'goodness'. Creativity is morally inert. Creativity can serve the 'good' end of the spectrum and it can serve the 'bad'.

****

We expose the flexibility and plasticity of our moral judgements when creative products, which we once viewed as scandalous, shift along the benefit spectrum and are elevated to great respect and value.

The repugnant, obscene and disgusting can, over time, become tame, decent – even beautiful. And of course, we must recognise that the good can just as easily become bad, by accident or intent. But where did this bad creativity come from?

We do not have to look too far.

We have already seen religion has a strong influence on our understanding of creativity. For thousands of years, creativity has been adopted by religions and presented as a mysterious behaviour that is linked with gods.

So, in malcreativity we have an apparent religious anomaly. If gods created the universe, if they are so benevolent and inherently good, who or what created these bad malcreative things?

Many religions would have us believe there is a god of 'badness'. This entity has travelled through the centuries under many guises, in many religions, but it is commonly thought of as some sort of devil.

We could discuss the logic of all-powerful gods that create opposite and opposing forces. As interesting as the argument may be, we can see these postulations were the products of a pre-Dark Ages intellect, struggling to make sense of a complicated world.

When these ideas were proposed we did not have the benefit of the centuries of discoveries about our universe, or the legion of alternative theories and opinions we have developed since then.

If you have a religious conviction, you may connect malcreativity– the 'bad stuff', with the work of some sort of devil. And creativity, the 'good stuff', with the work of some sort of god.

If you do not have a religion, you must recognise creativity is a behaviour that can be used to further Mankind's advancement, in the making of new inventions, discoveries and ideas. But it can also be used to inspire our worst behaviours, and generate our most unpleasant creative products.

When we are nasty to each other, we draw upon enormous quantities of malcreativity in our attempts to make our own lives better. In that process, we will often harm or destroy our opponents, enforce our beliefs [including our morals], and protect our cultures.

The reason why our cultures still exist, and others remain as interesting exhibits in our museums, is because our cultures overpowered previous cultures. We absorbed or destroyed them, using – amongst other things – our malcreativity. However, it is time in our evolution to make some difficult decisions.

We need to make that creative breakthrough. We need to stimulate the 'Aha!' moment. We need to spill the bath water and flood the floor.

When we invent new weapons and processes that maim and kill: new missiles that make orphans, behaviours that torture and starve – we are being malcreative.

When we find new ways to demolish cities, tear lives apart, incinerate children, we are creating our dim future with our malcreativity.

We have used our malcreativity, and we continue to use it, to make some individual lives better, often to the detriment of thousands of other lives.

In this process, we continue to use values, traditions, ideologies and morality that have been formed over millions of years.

But these entrenched genetic and behavioural traits – inherited from our ancestors – are no longer useful, many of them are dangerous.

When we consider the definition of creativity, should we exclude malcreativity? Should we twist the definition to eliminate bad behaviour? Should we censor some of our creativity because it makes us feel uncomfortable? Should we reject creativity that harms others, dismissing all the horrific malcreative products from our idea of creativity?

In our new understanding, should we define creativity as good and moral?

No!

We have to face up to the message.

We are all products of our past creativity – good and bad.

We have evolved by winning the creativity competition with other species, and with parts of our own species.

Someone had to sit down and use their creativity to conjure up a new way to eradicate the opposition, or improve the manner in which it was done previously.

We must assume our predecessors could have employed their creativity in some other way, that did not injure, maim, poison or kill. However, our ancestors chose to obey their most ignoble, most ancient and most human directives. They chose to behave with malcreative behaviour.

We are all the result of past humans that **chose** to use their malcreativity to invent better ways to be unpleasant, so they could survive a little longer: spears, swords, arrows, bombs, napalm, drones, chemical warfare, nuclear weapons. All of these creative products are the result of malcreative behaviour, set deep in the human psyche. All are inglorious expressions of Mankind's malcreative abilities.

The ancient rules of the evolutionary game state the winners will be those that can employ creativity best in the struggle to survive.

But those rules have changed.

As a species, we need to find a way of controlling our malignant behaviours. We need to plot a new course that understands, controls and diminishes our malcreativity.

Malcreative products are key ingredients in Mankind's evolution and survival.

And, in a sublime paradox, they might just be responsible for our demise.

Today, we are just one push of a perfectly designed button from a catastrophic disaster.

A gentle thrust, that is the culmination of billions of years of evolution and creativity.

It is only a question of time before someone, somewhere, decides they would prefer collective death to spending eternity as an exhibit in someone else's museum.

It is time we stopped denying our malcreativity.

We need to start talking about it and understanding it.

The moral spectrum of creativity, and the exposure of malcreativity, reveals the paucity of our understanding of the subject, and the scant vocabulary that accompanies it.

We must focus our creativity on what is good for our planet, our species, and the millions of other species in our worldwide ecosystem.

We need to use our creativity to quell our malcreativity. Most importantly, we need to stop ignoring our creativity.

2.6. EPHEMERAL CREATIVE PRODUCTS.

Many creative products last for a very long time entering the history books or museums and galleries as coruscating achievements of Mankind. These creative products are important valuable and serious stuff that can change our culture, and the way that we all live.

But creative products do not always have to be significant or have long-lasting cultural importance. Much creativity can be transient, temporary and sometimes trivial. In this category we find adverts, popular music, television shows, the magazine article, the never to be repeated recital, the impromptu performance, the funny observation.

These creative products, of fashion and fad, often pander to our need for a little fun. These creative products may be of high-benefit for a short while, and they may be the result of high-intensity creative behaviour, but they quickly shift down the benefit spectrum, to be forgotten or replaced by the next ephemeral creative product.

Some domains appear to be dependent upon these 'quick turnover' creative products. The world of popular culture is often the home to this kind of creativity. But it should be noted that the ephemeral creative product, that at first sight appears to be intended for a short life, can surprise us all and in time become a long-lasting, high-benefit creative product.

Many of our trenchant and enduring creative products are the result of creative behaviours, that at first sight might have appeared to be ephemeral.

Consider the way new words and phrases are generated. Often a new expression can be coined in a transitory moment; in a heated conversation, or unscripted rant. It can then be repeated and used by others, gaining high-benefit status, only to be replaced and forgotten about within a few weeks or months.

But it should be noted that occasionally these impromptu expressions can take on a life of their own, and last for generations, being passed on through families, communities and cultures.

The work of Shakespeare is jam-packed with creative products that were intended to entertain for a few seasons, yet many of his phrases have lasted for centuries.

However, others expressions have failed to make the leap from the page to our collective consciousness, they remain short-lived and ephemeral.

And of course, there are many other examples of ephemeral creative products, many we shall never be aware of because they only benefitted someone for a short time, before they were dropped from use and forgotten.

We need to recognise and validate ephemeral creativity. We need to be able to identify it, include it in our understanding, and consider it when we define creativity.

2.7. FAILED CREATIVITY.

In all of the popular ideas about creativity, nobody appears to recognise the most common creativity: the creativity that fails. This is an enormous arena of ignored creativity.

This creative behaviour fails to achieve any creative product.

However, just because someone failed in their creative ambition, or produces the wrong solution, it does not mean the behaviour that fashioned that failure was not creative.

Just as the person that returns from the sea without any fish is still fishing, or the cook that burns the cakes is still cooking. And just as the gardener whose crops get eaten by the pigeons is still gardening.

So, the person that attempts to be creative but fails is still **behaving** creatively.

As a society we do not recognise this behaviour as important, worthy of applause or investigation.

This is silly as it can be essential to any successful creativity that may follow it. After all, if a successful creative product takes twenty attempts, we can consider nineteen of those to be failed creative behaviour.

Should we assume the nineteen failures had no part to play in the success of the twentieth? And, therefore, the only creative behaviour was in the twentieth attempt.

That would not make sense.

Suppose I were to write a poem.

I spend weeks, maybe months, poring over every word: every nuance, every reference, every suggestion, every arcane symbol is recognised.

I employ high-intensity creative behaviour, pumping my innovation blood vessels to bursting point, only to produce a two-verse limerick that doesn't rhyme.

Would I be feted as the next poet laureate? Would I have publishers queuing around my word processor with blank cheques, ready to publish? Would many people benefit from my work?

Perhaps not – but I would have employed gut-wrenching creative behaviour.

How about my painting? I spend days, perhaps weeks, making sure the drawing is perfect, that the colours are tested and matched, that the composition is perfectly balanced, that the brushstrokes are... just so.

Only to produce a painting that makes the dog howl.

Once again, the intensity of the creative behaviour is excruciating – but no prizes here for the creative product.

What if I intend to create a new type of cake? I use oranges, lavender and rose petals. I research the recipe. I plan the method. I experiment with the baking. I grow the lavender. I steal the petals from my neighbour's garden at midnight, and I import the highest-grade oranges from California.

114

I organise a dinner party to launch the new creation, only to find the cake tastes like burnt flip-flops.

Even the famished crows do not peck.

Have I been creative?

Is it feasible to imagine that the product of my disastrous creative behaviour is not the limerick, the painting or the cake – but the knowledge that was gained in the failure?

When I eventually succeed, should we credit the failures in my success? In which case, can we view the knowledge gained in failed creative behaviour as another form of creative product?

Failure is a common result of creative behaviour, but how often do we applaud those that try and fail? When do we appreciate that failure can be an example of creative behaviour? Where are the awards for those that do not succeed?

Unfortunately, our cultures have evolved to think the behaviour of the unsuccessful is something that deserves to be ridiculed, laughed at and scorned.

Our combative and competitive culture has been built on the veneration of the successful, and the mockery of failure.

But I hope we are now seeing these negative attitudes are symptoms of our evolution and our social conditioning.

These are symptoms we need to re-assess and challenge, if we are to form a better understanding of creativity– and form better cultures.

2.8. CREATIVITY IN THE WRONG PLACE AND TIME.

Some creative behaviour is ignored because it happens in the wrong place, or at the wrong time.

Sometimes, more than one person finds the creative solution to a problem, but only one person gets acclaim for their creativity.

There are many examples of this phenomena. The one I use comes from my school days.

It is not a very well-known fact that I invented the hovercraft when I was in primary school. While 'messing about' in class, I managed to propel my writing paper from one side of the table to the other, just by puffing out my cheeks and blowing – no doubt accompanied by some sort of 'bottom noises'.

My friends were very impressed. I tried to explain to the teacher the importance of my discovery.

"If we took the principle and scaled it up, we could make cars that floated on air rather than use tyres, we could save a fortune in rubber."

I clearly remember having one of those bath-splashing moments of insight, so characteristic of spontaneous creative behaviour. However, the teacher was not impressed.

He explained wearily, *"It has already been done"*

and I should, *"Stop messing about"*

and I should, *"Get on with my work."*

So much for a creative education.

My creative behaviour was ignored because the principle behind my creative product had already been discovered and applied to the design and manufacture of the hovercraft. Consequently, few people benefited from my creative behaviour.

My creative behaviour has occurred in the wrong place, and at the wrong time. My creative behaviour had produced a low-benefit creative product, only beneficial to myself and a few bored school friends.

If my creative behaviour had been recognised, and given a little encouragement, I might have found a new method of transportation, or another use for waste paper. It may even have spurred an insight into the nature of energy!

And if my teacher had a better understanding of creativity, in particular the teaching of creative behaviour, I could have explored all sorts of interesting ideas.

Perhaps my teacher could have put me on the road to becoming an engineer, a paper technician or an inventor. A teacher that understood creativity might have turned my writing assignment into, '*How we can use air to save rubber.*'

But I had been beaten to the patent office by about twenty years; my chance for fame and fortune had happened before I was even born.

Instead, I am still puffing out my cheeks and making 'bottom noises' to amuse my friends.

Creative behaviour is frequently happening in the wrong place, or at the wrong time; consequently, it is not valued.

When we use creative behaviour to discover something that is already known to the general public, it is usually ignored, even criticised.

Worse, the person being creative may be thought of as a plagiarist, a charlatan – even a precocious brat. All because we used second-class stamps, were born too late or the teacher was having a bad day.

The creative behaviour has definitely taken place, but it is unnoticed – even derided and laughed at.

In traditional models of creativity, we tend to acknowledge the person that got to the solution first– the gold medallist– and we ignore those that receive the silver and bronze.

Perhaps I did not play a part in the invention of the hovercraft, but I was behaving creatively.

Once again, we need to be able to identify and validate this form of creativity.

2.9. CREATIVITY AND LEARNING.

In part one, I examined the teaching of creativity in the traditional school setting, and I concluded it was woefully inadequate. However, this does not mean creativity does not happen in school.

Indeed, as we shall see, all learning involves some level of creativity. But this creativity is usually ignored.

The next few anecdotes explore the various ways creative behaviour is used when we learn new information or skills.

****

We can identify the use of creative behaviour in the learning of simple information. 'The capital of France is Paris' is an example of this sort of information. The teacher communicates it, sometimes repeatedly, and the student is required to remember it. In the remembering, the student is obliged to create a place for the new information in their existing pattern of knowledge.

In simple terms, whenever we learn something new, we use creative behaviour to make fresh neural pathways in our brains.

In this way, what was once unknown to the student becomes known. The creation of a new understanding and memory is the creative product of learning.

The process is the same for the student as it is for the artist, the scientist, the designer, the inventor or anyone else that explores their unknown.

Admittedly, the activities of the student in learning new information must be the smallest expression of creative behaviour because the creative product is already in the public domain.

But we should recognise that learning the information involves some form of creative behaviour.

Here we can identify the essence of creativity: exploring the unknown.

At the very lowest expression of creativity, the student explores and learns about things they do not know—or cannot do— using creative behaviour.

This results in new knowledge, understanding or skills for the student – the creative product.

At this lowest level of creativity, the student's new creative product is known to many other people. [*The capital of France is Paris.*]

At the highest expression of creativity, the artist, inventor, scientist, musician also learns about things they do not know—or cannot do—using creative behaviour.

This also results in new knowledge, understanding or skills – this is the creative product of the artist, the inventor the scientist, the musician.

This new creative product is **not known** to anyone else: it may be a new painting, a new invention, a scientific discovery, a new piece of music.

Of course, we must recognise that the student employs a different and easier creative process when learning their new information because they have a teacher to lead them and to provide direction in their search for understanding.

Whereas the lone person, attempting to be unveil a creative product, using high-level creative behaviour, is often working on their own.

But we should appreciate the connection between the actions of both parties: they both use creative behaviour, even if the problem they are exploring and the solution they are attempting to find are of a different quality.

We should also recognise that the student can learn and retrieve the information with more clarity, and more effectively, by employing higher intensity creative behaviour.

In this instance, the learning of this simple information would be more effective if it were augmented with photographs of the Eiffel Tower, the sound of Parisian buskers, the language of France, the smell of French bread and coffee, along with stories about France and many other 'memory hooks.'

The more time and effort the student applies to the creative behaviour of learning, the quicker, stronger and more efficient the neural pathways become.

Higher intensity creative behaviour will form a 'stronger' creative product for the student, by creating more powerful neural pathways, so the information is easier to access and retrieve.

This relationship, between higher intensity creative behaviour and better learning, would be obvious to any teacher or student. However, what has not been obvious in the past is the connection between the simplest of learning and creative behaviour.

Consequently, this aspect of creativity has, traditionally, been ignored. We must ensure it is accounted for in our new understanding.

2.10. CREATIVITY AND JUGGLING.

Let's examine another example of creative behaviour in learning. This example is slightly different from the previous example as the teacher's role is less pronounced.

If I were to try and teach you how to juggle, I could tell you how to juggle, and I could alert you of some of the problems you may encounter when learning how to juggle. But ultimately, that is not going to work.

If you are going to learn how to juggle, you are going to have to take those three balls and start throwing them around.

During this process you will make mistakes, and you will experience frustration; you will try many different solutions. You are going to have to try hard, and you are going to have to persevere; you are going to have to invent a way to solve the problem of juggling. You will have to employ creative behaviour to create your complex web of knowledge, understanding and skills.

You are going to have to analyse the problems you encounter, and you are going to have to come to terms with abilities and knowledge currently unknown to you. You are going to have to retrieve your juggling balls from the fish tank, and deal with punching yourself in the face. You are going to have to search for the balls behind the refrigerator, and cope with all the picking up and bending over. In this way, slowly– throw by throw– you will create the fresh neural infrastructure that confers the ability to juggle.

Undoubtedly, your creative behaviour is going to fail many times, and you will experience the frustrations and challenges that often accompany creativity and learning. But with persistence, and by raising the intensity of your creative behaviour, the problem will eventually be solved. What was once unknown, will become known.

This is exactly the same process any person that is behaving creatively uses. However, once again, the creative product of this learning – the neural structure that facilitates juggling – is not seen as astounding by others, as lots of people can juggle, so the creativity involved is ignored.

The role of the teacher is to act as a facilitator –a guide – someone to introduce the problems, someone to sympathise, encourage and explain a method.

But introducing, sympathising, encouraging and explaining does not describe learning: it describes teaching. Learning how to juggle is something the student does internally, by struggling with the problem and by using creative behaviour

Traditionally, learning is seen as dependent upon innate aptitudes, intelligences, inherited gifts, interests and talents, but we can see from these examples that learning is primarily dependent on creativity.

Learning is the ability to use creative behaviour to struggle with, and explore what we do not know, with the aim of creating fresh neural pathways, understandings, memories, skills and products.

2.11. CREATIVITY AND THE QUADRATIC EQUATION.

There is another type of learning, similar to that used when learning the kinaesthetic skills of juggling that would be useful to examine. In this case, the juggling takes place in the head.

If you were taught how to solve quadratic equations, you would need to be introduced to a thought process. You would need to use creative behaviour to learn a series of solutions to a series of problems.

This process would enable you to solve similar problems without help from others. In other words, you would learn the thinking skills involved in solving quadratic equations.

Just like juggling the three balls, you will need to learn to throw and catch the ideas and thoughts, until you can get the process right.

Only now, retrieving the balls from the fish tank, punching yourself in the face, searching behind the refrigerator, happens internally–inside your head.

In this example, we can see there is a mix between accruing simple information, carving neural pathways, developing internal thinking skills and exploring your unknown.

The teacher cannot tell you, or force you, to think in the correct fashion to solve the problem.

The teacher cannot physically get inside your brain, to combine the chemicals, spark electrical impulses, and throw the ideas in the right sequence.

You, the student, have to create these from the inside using creative behaviour. Just like a painter searching for the right brushstrokes, the musician searching for the right chord, or the physicist searching for the right formula.

All the teacher can do is guide you, encourage you, and provide an environment in which these things are capable of being formed. Finally, the teacher can sympathise, when you get it wrong, give you clues, steer you, and support you through the process.

Learning how to solve the equation may involve the highest intensity of creative behaviour. However, the ability to solve quadratic equations will not impress many others, or be recognised as creative, as it does not fit into the traditional understanding of creativity, or traditional teaching methods.

Furthermore, because millions of people already know how to solve quadratic equations, your creativity will not appear on the evening news, or cause headlines in Maths Monthly, as the product of your creative behaviour is low-benefit and therefore destined to be ignored.

2.12. THE CREATIVITY OF SELF EDUCATION.

I have one more example of ignored creativity in the learning experience. This is a slightly stronger expression of creative behaviour that exposes the creative behaviour involved in self-education.

Imagine Lily is learning to ride a bicycle. She has not done this sort of thing before, and she has only seen someone ride a bike from distance. So, the initial attempts are messy. She wobbles along for a few turns of the peddle before ending up in the hedge or hospital.

What Lily needs is a teacher, parent or a friend – someone from the community – to teach her this traditional skill. However, this child, perhaps by inherent determination, innate willpower, fortitude, self-belief, naiveté, playful intuition; or because she is being ignored and forced to think for herself, decides she is going to learn how to ride her bike without help from anyone else.

She experiments a number of times. Perhaps by trembling along precariously. Perhaps, by occasionally keeping one foot on the ground. In this way, she slowly deconstructs the problem attempting and failing many times. Whatever process she uses, she manages, after a great deal of effort and application, to learn how to ride her bike.

How do we assess this behaviour? We can see these are no ordinary actions. In the circumstances, it is an amazing achievement. Lily has learnt, without help or intervention from a teacher – by trial, error, ingenuity and determination – how to perform a very difficult task. I would argue this child is showing great tenacity and perspicacity in the solving of a very challenging problem. This is a tremendous personal triumph.

Most importantly, I would also claim Lily has used creative behaviour. We may even describe it as high-intensity creative behaviour, depending upon how much time and effort Lily used to solve the problem. However, no Nobel Prize here–or exhibition at the Museum of Modern Art– just a big smile of satisfaction, and the admiration of her friends and neighbours.

From the casual outsider's perspective, she is like every other six-year-old that has learnt how to ride a bicycle. Nobody recognises the personal qualities and general cleverness that went into solving the problem.

Significantly, no one sees the ability to ride a bicycle as a particularly creative achievement. This is because her bike riding skill is of little benefit to anyone else.

In which case, we can say Lily's new skill is a low-benefit creative product.

Consequently, Lily is lucky to get a pat on the head and an extra fish finger from her mother when she comes in for tea.

We may wish to reject Lily's self-education as an example of creativity, as it lacks the customary, amazing 'original' creative product that solves a common problem, or enthrals the community.

Lily's achievement certainly isn't a traditional conception of creativity. However, as part of our new understanding of creativity, we need to recognise and give value to the creative behaviour component in Lily's bike riding adventure.

As you may imagine, this form of self-education is not reserved for young children, or bike riding. It is happening all the time, to all age groups, in all occupations, in all cultures – throughout history. And the creative behaviour involved in the process is frequently ignored.

As Lily learnt to ride her bike, she used creative behaviour to explore what she did not know in an effort to learn or achieve something new. Just like Picasso, just like Mozart, just like Einstein.

We need to ensure we recognise self-education in our new understanding.

Creativity is a basic ingredient of learning; learning is a basic ingredient of creativity.

2.13. EXTERNAL AND INTERNAL CREATIVITY.

We have examined some of the commonly held ideas about creativity, and we have recognised some of the unspoken and ignored presentations of creativity. But before I build upon these findings and propose a new definition, we must return to one last anomalous aspect of creativity that surfaced earlier: the relationship between creativity and entertainment.

The inspection of this relationship opens a whole new vista on the subject, and it exposes a range of observations that are incredibly important to our understanding.

So far, I have portrayed creativity as a wide-ranging and fundamental part of Mankind's character. We can see that creativity has been integral to Mankind's history and development. But how does this square up to the fact that the biggest consumer of creative behaviour is focused on, what appears to be, our least vital activities: sports, art, music, singing, dancing, games, humour, storytelling? Many observers cite these domains of entertainment when they think of creativity, or when they are trying to characterise it. This is confusing.

At first sight, entertainment and survival appear incompatible. One seems frivolous and light-hearted, focused on enjoyment and fun. The other is essential and deadly serious, concentrated on life and death problems. Both appear to rely on creativity for their efficacy and validity.

To understand the connection between survival behaviour and entertainment, we must examine and appreciate the evolution of creativity in Mankind. For this understanding, we must assume the ancestral creatures that early Mankind evolved from were not as creative as modern humans, and our early creative behaviour was exclusively concentrated on solving the essential problems of survival and maintaining life.

In the beginning, we used our creativity to invent, clothes, cooking, fire, shelters, weapons, hunting, farming, politics, social structures, medicine. But what happened after we have satisfied all of our base survival needs, and we found ourselves sitting round the evolutionary campfire, twiddling our thumbs, picking our teeth and whittling sticks?

What did we do with all the spare time? As humans evolved, we applied some of our creative behaviour to making our lives more fun and meaningful.

We developed cultures that meant we did not have to spend all our time hunting for the next meal, chasing the opposite sex, and getting into fights with other tribes. [Although, many still try.] Once we learnt how to solve the essential problems of survival, and we temporarily had no *external* problems or worthy challenges from the outside world …. we got bored. To fill that challenge vacuum, Mankind engaged with *internal* problems: problems that come from our own minds. We invented problems to satisfy our boredom and entertain our novelty-addicted brains.

We told stories, we danced, we painted cave walls, we made jewellery and decorated clothes, we experimented with the things we ate, we competed against each other, and played games – we invented new domains beyond those of survival.

In other words, after we had used creativity to solve the external problems of life that would improve the *quantity* of our lives, we used creativity to solve the internal problems of our minds, to improve the *quality* of our lives, by entertaining each other.

And, as our survival rates improved, and the size of our brains increased, we incrementally extended the amount of time spent on these new domains. Here is another essential dichotomy of creativity. We can form a spectrum of external and internal creativity to illustrate this.

SPECTRUM OF EXTERNAL / INTERNAL CREATIVITY.	
EXTERNAL PROBLEMS --------------INTERNAL PROBLEMS	
Survival	Entertainment
Early Humans	Modern Mankind
Quantity of survival	Quality of survival
Natural	Man-made

Today, we can locate any problem, or domain of problems, on this spectrum – with the bulk of them, in the middle of the spectrum, containing a mixture of external and internal problems.

Perhaps this simple division sounds superficial. Perhaps we should reason that the new light-weight domains of entertainment would not affect, or contribute to, our survival and evolution. Therefore, they would not appear to be a serious factor in the ascent of our species.

But we should be more perceptive than this: we can infer this 'non-essential', internal creativity provided something more than simple entertainment, and they had a function beyond satisfying our boredom and improving the quality of our spare time.

Entertainment could also impact upon our ancestor's longevity. These new cultural domains: the ability to sing, make jokes, tell stories and play games, would help tribes to bond and support one another when the primary drive of survival got tough. We can imagine the early human would have preferred to belong, stay with, and fight for a community that had a stronger and more interesting culture. Rather than give way or defect to another tribe with a less stimulating and less entertaining existence.

In this depiction of prehistoric culture, the best tribes would have attracted the best brains and characters to support and fight for the best lifestyles.

The tribe that played together, stayed together – and survived together.

In this way, we can imagine these new cultural domains of entertainment improved the survival rate of the community.

We can push this idea further: the division between external and internal problems accounts for a much more modern separation – the tenuous creative partition between science and the arts.

The primary focus of science is learning about the world around us, dealing with the external problems coming from outside our minds: from our natural environment. The scientific domains employ creativity to try to discover the essential properties of our world, with the aim of improving our understanding of the universe and our place in it.

This scientific understanding attempts to improve the length, or quantity, of our lives– and extend our life chances.

In contrast, the focus of internal domains is the exploration of the entertainment value of our creativity, with the intention of improving the quality of our lives, by inventing solutions to the problems that we generate from within our minds.

Put over-simply, science employs creativity to *discover*; art employs creativity to *invent*.

There are further observations worth noting. The solutions to external problems are often assessed objectively, and the solutions to our internal problems are often assessed subjectively.

Scientific solutions to our problems are not opinions but facts. These are the tenets of the scientific domains.

Scientific solutions can be proven against the hard physical, biological and chemical problems of the external world that we all have to contend with.

Whereas many of the problems that come from within our minds are subjective. These are the problems we recognise as individuals: the problem and solutions we often 'play with' in our arts and entertainments.

We cannot prove the solutions to these personal 'mind' problems have any benefit outside our individual sensibility. If you do not find benefit in the music, the painting or the novel, it is rarely any good explaining it or trying to prove it is 'right'.

We can take this observation further: occasionally, we are challenged to study an internal problem that considers a much higher, and a much deeper, level of problem.

Sometimes the domains of entertainment go beyond the cursory, the ephemeral and the superficial.

When the arts are most profound, they transcend simple entertainment, to communicate deeper and more sensitive messages.

In this way, they can pose fundamental questions, and carry vital solutions, that allow us to scrutinise our unique behaviours, our most personal thoughts, and our most private, far-reaching fears.

Once Mankind had started to invent problems and solutions for our entertainment, we progressed to asking some of those more pertinent internal questions.

Why are we here?

What happens when we die?

How should we live our lives?

Is this all there is?

What is creativity?

Is there something else?

How did we get here?

Why do we behave the way we do?

In other words, Mankind started to ask– small, and then big– philosophical questions.

Once Mankind had become used to playing games with balls, arrows, sounds, colours, shelters and foods, we moved on to playing games with ideas.

When these internal questions are at their most interesting, they lead us to examine the nature of our individual humanity, our place in our culture, and this universe.

These advanced personal questions describe the tertiary evolutionary function of creativity and entertainment: self-examination – a combination of science, art and philosophy.

Therefore, we can propose an evolving application of creativity in Mankind: the primary role of survival, the secondary role of entertainment and the tertiary role of philosophy.

An interesting further observation of this spectrum is the contrasting impact it has on our species in contrast to the individual.

At one end of the spectrum, the essential nature of survival means the external problems of survival affect the whole species.

External problems tap into a primal human homogeneity we all feel: we all want freedom from pain and to stay alive.

External problems deal with our similarities.

External problems are problems for all of us.

The whole species recognise these problems: thirst, hunger, fatigue, fear, illness, death, gravity.

Consequently, the creative products that result from these problems often become our long lasting high-benefit products: medicine, fire, food, shelter, science – the stuff we all need.

The secondary qualities of entertainment appear less vital to the community: they chime with the accumulated culture of the individual human being.

Our internal problems find solutions that communicates with, and generally benefits, smaller numbers of people.

The appreciation of the Statue of Liberty, choral music or tweed is subjective: only of benefit to a sub-division of humanity. And the questions of personal philosophy can be a very individual matter: each of us have to find the answers that form our own, sometimes unique, perception of our environment, and our lives.

From birth we are required to cobble together our own understanding – our own philosophy – based upon our own unique experiences. We form our own bespoke reality and understanding of life, to sustain us in our own exclusive – but often very similar – environment.

As befitting behaviours that have evolved over hundreds of thousands of years, these divisions of creativity are not distinct or exclusive. Most of the time, we can identify primary, secondary and tertiary factors in any creative behaviour or creative product.

But these factors are distinct enough to be worth noting, and they are different enough for us to examine their properties, and to talk about them. Moreover, we can use them to better understand the driving forces of our individual behaviours, along with the various complexions of human creativity, and the societies we belong to. We need to recognise the chronological development of creativity, and the distinct functions of these various stages, so we can represent them in our new understanding, our new vocabulary, and our new definition of creativity.

PART THREE

A NEW UNDERSTANDING OF CREATIVITY.

In Part One, we examined the old fashioned, traditional ideas about creativity, to reveal some startling anomalies and incongruities.

In Part Two, we uncovered some of the hidden and ignored aspects of creativity.

In Part Three, we shall build our new understanding on these foundations and provide a workable definition of creativity.

3.1. A NEW DEFINITION OF CREATIVITY.

Before I propose a new definition of creativity, and expand upon our new understanding, it would be useful to remind ourselves of some of our findings, and revisit some of the new terminology.

Firstly, we dispelled the idea that creative is limited to a few small parts of human activity – commonly called domains. Then we dismissed the old ideas that creativity is a rare and supernatural talent that only a few gifted people are party to.

Next, we established that creativity is composed of two distinct entities: creative behaviour and the creative product. By exploring this division, we opened up new perspectives. This includes low-intensity creative behaviour and the low-benefit creative product.

These observations led us to a new understanding of the relationship between learning and creative behaviour, and we recognised that there is a division between creativity applied to external problems and the creativity we apply to internal problems: between the creativity of science – that discovers, and the creativity of art – that invents.

Also, we have unveiled a 'dark side' to creativity: malcreativity – the stuff responsible for many of the bad creative products of Mankind. Along with this, we have identified a number of different expressions of creativity: small creativity, failed creativity, ephemeral creativity, pretend and authentic creativity

From all this, we can see it is possible to 'mix and match' these various presentations using new vocabulary.

We can identify and talk about small malcreativity, and we can visualise the low-benefit creative product that is the result of medium-intensity creative behaviour.

We can imagine the low-benefit malcreative product that fails, the medium-benefit creative product that employs low-intensity creative behaviour, that eventually becomes the failed creative product. Along the way, we have significantly increased our understanding of creativity and the vocabulary we can use to discuss this broad subject.

But what is the common denominator in these many categories? What binds all of these examples of creativity? And where are the boundaries? In other words, how do we define creativity?

My definition of creativity is not restricted to discrete areas of human activity, nor is it dependent upon gods, supernatural powers or other mystical entities for its efficacy. It does not require suspicious substances that unlock your 'mojo' and make you want to dance with the vicar, and it does not require you to suffer from a mental illness.

My definition locates creativity as a potential in all people and is applicable to all domains. But here is the problem with defining creativity: it is such a ubiquitous, universal, pervasive entity it has become infused in our lives, in our thoughts and our collective psyche.

On one level it is very simple – we do it naturally – like listening, walking or digestion. We do not need to understand it for it to function. It is embedded in our characters, our biology, our most modern fads and our most ancient of cultures. Consequently, it is a much more common behaviour than traditional thinking about creativity suggests.

We can see creativity is responsible for our highest achievements, but it is also to blame for many of our most shameful behaviours. It can make small changes to our individual lives, and it can be responsible for wonderful discoveries that change the world. It can entertain us for a few seconds, and it can improve the life expectancy of the whole species. Most importantly, it can fail spectacularly.

Although, historically, we have been misled and misdirected about the nature of creativity. We can now see that creativity always tries to explore what we do not know in an attempt to change our world and make our lives better. We do this when designing a new bomb, and when we are learning how to spell.

Therefore our definition:

Creativity is a spectrum of behaviour that attempts to explore our unknown with the aim of learning something new or solving a problem.

Here we have our definition that we can use to explore the outer reaches and deepest sanctums of creativity. This is the flag we need to salute or burn.

It should not be too contentious: it is broad enough to be inclusive and brief enough to use. It covers all of the presentations and categories of creativity, but most importantly, it works – and it makes sense.

But it is not enough.

By itself, the definition does not provide a comprehensive understanding of creativity: just as knowing the chemical composition of water does not describe the full variety of ways it can display itself to us, or its many uses.

The definition is a good starting point, but it poses many questions. We still have to refine our understanding of problems. We still have to explore other spectrums of creativity. We have to ask – what makes one creative product more creative than another?

We need to examine the significance of the word 'attempt' in the definition. We have to find out why some creativity succeeds and other creativity fails. We need to decide what should be done about malcreativity?

We shall find, as we explore this creative landscape, this map has been folded very tightly. The task now is to uncrease it, smooth it, examine it, explore it and try to understand it. We need to become familiar with this new place, at all hours of the day, from all compass points and in all seasons.

3.2. THE PROBLEMS OF PROBLEM SOLVING.

In the definition and my observations, I have made a firm connection between creative behaviour and problem solving. There is nothing controversial in this, many commentators have made a similar connection. Many cite problem solving as the sole function of creativity. There is a lot of truth in this idea. However, there are anomalies that need exploring and straightening out, before it can make sense.

****

The link between creativity and problem solving is easy to make when the problem is obvious and the process for solving the problem is clear. Designing and making a new type of teapot, or writing an amusing speech for a wedding reception, are excellent examples of the sort of activity that require creativity.

This type of 'brief-led' problem solving is very common. It represents the most conscious and objective form of creativity; consequently, it is an easy process to understand.

For some, this is where creativity starts and finishes: someone recognises a problem, a brief is formed – the instructions for the job – then the brief is completed, presumably using some level of creative behaviour.

Everything is well-defined and easy to understand. However, creativity and problem solving is not always as straight forward as this.

Brief setting is great when we can identify and describe a problem easily, perhaps in a scientific or design domain that deals with a problem of the external environment: devise a new ship powered by seawater, a clothes peg that whistles when it rains, a cure for baldness. Learn how to ride a bicycle.

But some problems are much more difficult to recognize, particularly when dealing with internal problems that are difficult to articulate because the problem is personal and emanates from the mind.

Because of this, many observers reject the idea that creativity is solely to do with problem solving. They cannot make the connection with creativity and difficult to identify internal problems. After all, what problem does a poem, a painting or a piece of music solve? What is the brief? Who is setting it?

In addition, often the person working in an artistic domain will reject the idea they are solving a problem. They say, when they create something, they are doing 'what comes naturally' – or they are doing it because they have to – they are just responding to their inquisitiveness. Some even say creativity is a mystery that does not tolerate investigation. But often the person attempting to be creative acts without understanding the influences on their behaviour.

Just because someone is behaving creatively does not mean they understand the process: just as we do not have to understand how oxygen affects the body for us to benefit from breathing it, or understand the mechanics of a microwave oven for us to use it.

Humans have evolved to behave creatively – when required. Consequently, much creative behaviour happens intuitively– without conscious understanding.

This shaky connection between problem solving and creativity is exacerbated when we consider more mundane problems.

How do we get to the police station?

How do we drive a bus?

Should I eat the lemon drizzle cake or the pizza?

How do these sorts of problems fit into the idea that creativity is problem solving?

In answering these problems, we can be creative, but more often we are not. If creativity is problem solving, why do some problems not need creativity to solve them?

Moreover, how do we solve most of the problems of daily life without creativity? Two plus two is a problem. But how can we say we use creativity in solving it? After all, everyone knows the answer: so, it is not much of a problem.

Furthermore, the answer is not very creative. Unless we make the answer 37 – but that's a book from a different library.

In addition, should we always aspire to creative behaviour when faced with a problem? As we have seen elsewhere, most of the time we do not use creativity to solve the difficulties of life.

There are good reasons for this.

Do we really want a creative helicopter pilot, looping-the-loop before landing, or a creative dentist filling cavities with candyfloss and fitting green false teeth? Nouvelle cuisine can be wonderful, but sometimes we just want good old-fashioned, uncreative, stomach-filling stew.

So, what do we call problem solving behaviour that is not creative?

Because we cannot identify an easy connection between all creative behaviour and all problem solving, some assume creativity only has a fragile link with problems solving. Even that problem solving only relates to some sorts of creativity. In which case, problem solving cannot really be a defining feature of creativity.

This is confusing.

It appears, creativity has a lot to do with problem solving. However, it seems some problems require creativity to solve them, and others do not. And sometimes, the last thing we need is a creative solution to the problem.

If we are to improve our understanding of creativity, we must first investigate the nature of problems – and the behaviour we use to solve them.

To understand creative behaviour, and its relationship with problem solving, there is a basic principle we must adopt.

All behaviour is an attempt to solve a problem.

From conception to death – day in, day out – we spend our lives solving problems. We do this to stay alive and make our lives better.

Generally, we do not recognise this principle.

Generally, we think problems are occasional interruptions of an otherwise trouble-free and harmonious life.

Generally, we define a problem as an awkward situation that causes us concern and makes us think hard to overcome it.

Apparently, problems need to be challenging if we are to consider them a problem.

However, these noticeable and irritating problems are just a small number of the continuous and vast array of problems we encounter in our lives.

Problems can range from the most easy to the brain splinteringly difficult.

Problems can be arranged by their difficulty on a spectrum.

THE SPECTRUM OF PROBLEMS

EASY PROBLEMS-----------------------DIFFICULT PROBLEMS

Very common Problems	Very Rare problems
Easy to solve	Hard to solve
Least thought and effort	Most thought and effort
Not noticed	Noticed

The easy to solve problems are located to the left of the spectrum. These problems are solved using some of our oldest behaviours.

We can think of these old behaviours as the automatic pilot of our lives, responsible for the problems we face in the maintenance of our bodies.

These behaviours keep us alive without need for interference from thought or conscious brain. These behaviours solve our most essential problems: when resting, asleep, even when in a coma.

These ancient problems are the most basic of life: breathing, yawning, excreting, sleeping, the circulation of blood, digesting, moving, blinking and growing. We have evolved efficient behaviours to solve these problems.

These behaviours are so essential to our survival that we do not need to learn them: we inherit them from our parents through our genes.

We share many of these problems and easy solutions with other species. We solved many of these problems as nascent organisms – right at the start of life on earth – when the evolutionary tree was just a sapling.

Evolution, and the constant repetition of a life-sustaining solution, have 'hardwired' these behaviours into our morphology and our biology.

Along with the easy to solve survival problems– that we have genetic answers to – we have more difficult problems.

We use creativity to learn the solutions to these problems from other people, as part of our socialisation process – and as part of our education.

As we mature, we encounter bigger problems that require a more conscious behaviour. Who should I marry? Should I confess? What house should I buy? Should I go to the doctor?

These, less easy to solve problems, can cause a lot of conscious thought and worry. These problems are located in the middle of the spectrum. They form the bulk of our conscious lives.

Then there are the really annoying problems: the ones that keep us awake at night, and can dominate our thoughts. These troublesome problems are situated to the right of the spectrum. Each problem, however easy or difficult to solve, affects our thoughts and our behaviours.

Our days are filled with many small problems, scattered with a generous smattering of medium-sized problems, along with a small selection of the more challenging ones.

Our lives are sustained, and made better, when we find the behaviours that solve them. When we solve problems well, we thrive – our lives get better. When we get the answers wrong, our lives get worse.

As you can imagine, there are thousands of individual behaviours we use to solve the problems in our lives; however, for our purposes, we only need to identify two categories of problem-solving behaviour: conventions and creativity.

Let's examine conventions first.

3.3. SOLVING PROBLEMS WITH CONVENTIONS.

Conventions are reliable, tried and tested, problem-solving behaviours. Mostly, they are learnt or inherited from other people. The use of conventions to solve problems accounts for the vast majority of our behaviour.

There is no objective way of establishing what the majority is in numerical terms. However, as a rough guide, I suggest over ninety-seven percent of our behaviour uses conventions.

There are very good reasons why we use so many conventions: conventions are the easiest, quickest and most reliable solution to the problems we encounter. Usually, we do not have to think too hard about how to use them. Normally, conventions are sure to work.

By using a convention, we do not have to create a new solution to a problem – we just repeat one we have used before, or copy one from someone else. Consequently, conventions are the most energy efficient method of solving a problem.

There are a many different names for the conventions we use: habits, tropes, reflexes, traditions, memes, mores, customs, rituals, beliefs and laws. Our societies, cultures and civilisations are founded, and are sustained, by the use of many long-standing conventions.

Along with these behavioural conventions, we have the conventional information that informs them.

This information is sometimes called conventional wisdom. This is facts and knowledge that has already been established to be true, and that that most of us agree upon. Conventional wisdom is the stuff that is taught in our educational institutions.

This conventional wisdom is the accrued knowledge of our society and our ancestors, and it comprise the status quo of our understanding. We rely upon this knowledge when conducting our lives.

INNATE CONVENTIONS.

Our most resilient solutions to the problems of living are inherited. The oldest and most vital conventions are passed on from a long list of antecedents that stretch right back to the first signs of life on Earth.

These genetic conventions have been refined by evolution, in response to the problems our species has faced over the millennia.

Successful genetic conventions are promoted through natural selection. Those conventions that help us to survive are kept and repeated. Those conventions that hinder survival eventually become redundant and are 'dropped'.

In this way, the environments and problems our forebears faced, and the behaviours they used to solve those problems, have shaped our present-day biology and morphology.

With these birthday gifts, provided by our ancestors, we are born into a world of other people's conventions.

LEARNT CONVENTIONS.

As we grow, we are taught and copy the best behavioural conventions. We constantly watch the behaviours of other people. As we monitor, we are evaluating, testing, and assessing each convention. Conventions are responsible for our morals, beliefs, values, skills, knowledge, mannerisms and attitudes. Our collection of conventions become our personality and our character.

If we experience a better solution to a problem, we copy that solution. In this way, we collect conventions from a broad circle of social environments. Our constant aim is to make our lives better. The longer we survive: the more problems we encounter. Conventions can be diverse and complex: an attitude, a method of travelling to work, a piece of clothing, the food we eat, the words we speak, our politics, our thoughts on the economy.

Across the world there are billions of conventions that can be learnt. As individuals we only need to learn the ones that are useful to us, in the environment we inhabit.

By copying the behaviour of those around us, we show respect to indigenous people and their conventions. In this way, we acknowledge our similarities.

By repeating other people's behaviour, we pay an implicit compliment to the rest of the community. We all laugh at the same thing. We all follow the same team. We all use the same language. We have similar experiences, similar memories – similar problems.

We feel empowered by the support of people that have a similar mind, body, behaviour. When we do things together, we feel safe. Common problems and common conventions bond communities.

Communities come in many sizes and forms: the family, the village, the city, the business, the workplace, religion, the political party, the nation; all are founded and are bound by common conventions.

When someone refuses to abide by a convention they can offend people in the community. Just proposing a new idea, or a new way of doing things, can cause conflict. Behaving differently can be seen as a rebuke to others. By wearing different clothes, speaking in a different way, or developing new work methods, we can annoy members of the community. Even the smallest deviation from conventional behaviour can upset people – sometimes slightly, sometimes greatly. There is strong communal pressure to stick with established conventions.

The common use of behavioural conventions communicates that we share a mutual experience of the environment. The use of the same or similar behaviours is an acknowledgement that we face similar challenges. In this way, each use of a convention is a potential connection, a communication that reaches out to make a link with others. Each pristine, unchanged convention is a message: it proves we are the same or similar, and we can rely on this behaviour to solve our problem. Even if it is just for that one glorious moment when, the chords are struck, the goal is scored, the hunger is sated.

All this might suggest that we do not have a choice in the conventions we use, and that we are just passive receivers of conventions. This is partially true. Certainly, genetic conventions are passed onto us without consultation from our parents. And we rarely think about, or realise, the process we go through when we are educated in the conventions of a community.

Even if we recognise the influences, there is little we can do to avoid the conventions that surround us. We get little say in the environment we are exposed to as a young child, and we are not encouraged to question the status quo. Consequently, we can identify a large measure of passive indoctrination in the accrual of conventions.

However, because each of us is genetically unique, and each of us is exposed to a unique environment, we each have a different experience and perception of the world. We each perceive a different set of problems, and we each search for and accumulate our own personal solutions to solve those problems.

As a result, we each form a distinctive, eclectic collection of behavioural solutions from the range of conventions that we are exposed to.

This process makes us all unique......but similar.

3.4. SOLVING PROBLEMS WITH CREATIVITY.

Now we have established we can view all behaviour as problem solving, and the vast majority of behaviour uses conventions that have been copied from other people, we can at last examine the counterpart of conventions, and the main focus of our enquiry: the use of creative behaviour to solve problems.

This explanation is supported by a simple diagram.

The Circle of Conventions.

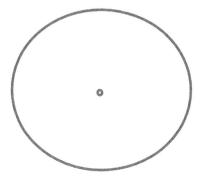

The circle is full of all the conventions I have accumulated in my life. The circle is filled with the bright light of conventional wisdom. Outside the circle is everything unknown to me. Outside the circle is where unconventional solutions lie. Outside the circle are solutions that have to be accessed by using creative behaviour.

The most effective way to understand creativity, and its relationship with conventions, is to work through a simple problem.

Suppose I have an itch on the end of the nose...

The itch is a simple and very common problem. Often, it would be solved without thinking: with a tip of a finger. This first attempt to solve the problem comes from the genetic conventions I inherited in the womb. These primordial solutions are located in the centre of my circle of conventions.

However, if my innate conventions do not solve the problem, I shall have to try a learnt convention: a convention I have acquired since birth.

Perhaps I could find relief for my itch by bathing my nose in some water, or by putting an ice cube on it. Maybe I can use a more modern convention: I could put some proprietary ointment on it from the medicine cabinet. Maybe I should try my grandmother's garlic and honey poultice?

Each time I fail to find an answer, I have to put a bit more time and effort into trying to solve the problem, and I have to use a little more mental and physical energy. Each new attempt to solve the problem requires me to move outwards, from the centre of the circle, and closer to the circumference of the circle. Here, on the outskirts, my least dependable and newer conventions are stored.

I feel very safe in the convention circle. In here, I am happy, secure, confident. In here, I can be smug and self-satisfied. Also, on occasion, I feel a little bored and unchallenged. In here, I **know** the answers to life's problems. I do not need to guess, ponder, worry or think – too hard.

In my circle of conventions, others surround me; they are agreeable. They behave like me and speak like me. They are members of my community. They have similar conventions. They huddle me on all sides. However, I have a unique problem. I have an itchy nose – and the itch will not go away.

My close community suggest I visit a doctor. Doctors spend years accumulating medical conventions from all over the world – from the ancient to the most modern. From the trusted to the most precarious.

Tests are conducted, samples taken, questions asked, drugs trialled, concoctions smeared. Many attempts are made to find a convention that will stop my nose itching. But nothing solves the problem.

Nothing stops my itch.

In desperation, I decide to do some research of my own. I sign up for evening classes in Amateur Pharmacology. I am going to learn all I can about 'itchy snitches' in the hope I can find a convention that will solve my problem.

Now, with the aid of the diagram of the circle of convention, we can clearly see the relationship between creativity and learning that we explored in part two.

Whenever we attempt to learn something new, we go to the furthest extent of our circle of conventions to explore our unknown. In the learning process, we employ creative behaviour with the aim of forging new neural pathways, and new understandings.

In essence, the accrual of new neural pathways expands my stock of existing conventions. This learning activity happens on the circumference of my circle of conventions. It is here – on the border of what I know– that learning takes place.

Here is a graphic illustration of the interplay between creativity and conventions in the learning process. When learning, we use creative behaviour to explore our personal unknown.

Unfortunately, in this case the learning is unsuccessful. The existing community conventions fail to supply the answer to my problem. Consequently, I am forced to increase the intensity of my creative behaviour.

****

Now I am standing at the extremes of the things I know. I am staring-out to the limitless depths of my unknown. Out there, in the dark shadows there is no order or system, just shifting shapes.

Out there, the half-light stores everything I do not know. Out there, are all of my malformed conventions, mutant ideas, strained thoughts and mongrel notions– the stuff of dreams and the semi-subconscious. Here lie the twilight thoughts that divide the community from the individual – the normal from the abnormal – the strange from the familiar. Because these obscured concepts are alien and ill-defined, they scare me, but the fear releases a charge of anticipation through my body.

Perhaps in the gloom I shall find satisfaction? Perhaps in here I shall find my solution: the answer to my problem?

If I want to solve my problem, I have to take the risk, I have to step over the circumference of the circle and explore this new place.

At this point I have tried all my conventions. I have asked my community to search their own circles of convention. I have questioned medical experts. I have learnt all of the existing conventions of the subject.

I have used up the 97% of conventional problem-solving behaviours. Now, I must start on the remaining 3%. I have to stop searching for an answer with a convention. I have to start using creative behaviour.

****

My first attempts at finding a solution involve low-intensity creative behaviour.

I pick at a few ideas and examine obvious possibilities. I look for a quick and easy answer. But with each failure I am forced to venture forward, away from the circle of conventions, into the dark unknown of higher-intensity creative behaviour.

My senses are tingling. Everything is unfamiliar. Everything is new. Everything is a potential threat or a possible solution. My brain is racing as I try to establish which is which. I feel strange. I feel more alive. I am being creative.

167

Back in my circle of conventions, some of my community are annoyed with me. Some say my behaviour is odd. They are calling me obsessive and weird for worrying about my problem.

They say, I should put up with the problem – this is just the way life is – we all have unsolved problems we have to live with.

We are all surrounded by our fears. We are all bound by the darkness of the infinite unknown.

There are no maps for this place – no protocols, no etiquette, no modus operandi. I want to get out of here as soon as possible. I want to obey my fears. I want to find an answer to my problem. I want to get back to my convention circle and be 'normal' again.

I instinctively grope for possible solutions– picking up one thing, then another – sometimes examining things that have no logical connection to my problem.

I explore two, three, even four solutions at once – juggling them, banging them together, trying to make them work.

As I play; I make mistakes. I consider and reconsider everything. I fumble, with little to guide me. The process is haphazard and random.

I am being buffeted by my environment. I being pushed and pulled– back and forth.

I am trying to find something to hold onto – anything to create a more stable situation.

I am searching for a solution that solves my problem.

Just like those initial chemicals – adrift in the broiling, crashing oceans. Just like those first cells, thrown by the tide.

Just like those earliest of organisms crawling onto the damp shore. Just like those ancient creatures creeping down from the trees.

Each failed attempt produces fresh insight.

Each failure, each grope, each slipped link, each surge into the unknown, causes me to learn something new – and takes me a little closer to a solution.

The more I search – the longer I spend in the creativity zone – the more confident I feel. The act of searching feels right, even when I am failing: it gives me hope.

It makes sense of the stultifying impotence of the circle of conventions. It satisfies my cloying frustration with the status quo. The tangled absurdity of this dark space appears to balance with the blinding cloud of righteous light found in the circle of conventions.

This is a completely different form of behaviour. This is a new sort of problem-solving. A new way of thinking. Now I have to rid myself of conventions. I have to accept the stinging light does not help. The gleaming conventions make the shadows darker, more solid.

Out in the creativity zone, I *have* to think differently. I *have* to look with new eyes, listen with new ears, feel with new skin. I *have* to think with new thoughts. I *have* to behave creatively.

Nobody has taught me how to behave out here, or what to expect. At school this area was completely out of bounds.

I was taught to stick with conventions, and be 'sensible', because that is where all the answers lie.

At school I was chastised for wasting time in the creativity zone: for daydreaming, for playing games, for messing about, for speculating. I was told this 'daydreaming' was a waste of time. There are no answers to exam questions across the circumference. All the exam questions have conventional answers that have to be learnt from someone else. Consequently, I have been trained – forced – to spend my life endlessly sifting through existing answers, never breaching my circumference.

I have been limiting my thoughts to stuff that is already known. My community has directed me to ignore this second place, to fear it – even to despise it.

****

I have to try to free myself from the known and work with what I do not know. I have to recognise the mysterious should not be feared. I have to embrace the irrational and the absurd.

Out here, in the creativity zone, I am forced to peer into places I cannot dream of. Out here, I shall question the most forbidding parts of my life. The dark of the unknown is the shadow of unanswered questions: that vast ludicrous absurdity that surrounds us.

That soft stone sponge blackness

outside of our understanding

and deep within us all.

3.5. WHAT DOES CREATIVE BEHAVIOUR LOOK LIKE?

How do I behave when I cross the circumference of the conventions circle? How do I respond when I step into the darkness? What qualities should I take into the creativity zone?

If we can answer these questions, we could recognize the characteristics we need to develop to improve our creativity. Most importantly, we could start to understand the qualities and features of creative behaviour.

DETERMINATION?

Perhaps determination is an important quality for someone who intends to explore the unknown and behave creatively. The ability to persevere with the search for an answer, in the darkness of the creativity zone, would seem like a valuable asset.

There is no doubt, finding an answer to a difficult problem, located deep in the creativity zone, will require high-intensity creative behaviour. In which case, determination would seem to be a very useful characteristic to have.

But creativity does not have to employ high-intensity creative behaviour to succeed. Often, we can find solutions by accident. We can find an answer by standing on the circumference and peering into the shadows, or by daydreaming. It is possible to be very creative just by wandering absent-mindedly into the dark place and getting lost.

Sometimes, we can find an easy solution just by placing two anomalous conventions next to each other on the circumference to spur an incongruous thought, or an abnormal relationship. Such lucky combinations – and easy, low-intensity, creative behaviour – accounts for vast quantities of creative products. Serendipity and creativity can be intimate bedfellows. In which case, we can say determination may be necessary for the most difficult to solve problems, but it is not essential for all creativity.

KNOWLEDGE.

Having a good knowledge of the existing conventions of a domain would be an asset when trying to be creative. This may be most useful in the early stages of low-intensity creative behaviour, when the solution to the problem is located just outside the circumference, in the half-light of the creativity zone.

When trying to solve a problem by exploring the unknown, we may imagine it would be valuable to be aware of the existing conventions. This would stop us wasting too much time and effort inventing a solution that has already been discovered. In addition, knowledge of existing conventions would allow us to change, tinker and adapt small parts of the convention in my quest to find an answer.

For example, if I were to write a creative piano concerto, we may imagine the ability to play the piano would be a useful attribute. I would be able to inspect and adjust the existing solutions in the crepuscular light, just across the circumference of my conventions. This is the process many people, steeped in the conventions of a domain, use when they are being creative.

However, when we come to creativity in the dark depths of the creativity zone, the ability to let go of conventions, and to work outside of the preconceptions of the status quo, would allow me a total freedom.

We can imagine if I had never written a piece of music for the piano, a complete ignorance – coupled with intense determination – might, in the right conditions, produce an extremely creative piece of music.

Perhaps it would not appeal to the purist, or those that venerate the craft of the domain; nevertheless, we can appreciate it could be very interesting, and may be very creative.

****

But, as we have seen elsewhere, extreme originality, devoid of all convention, will not necessarily result in something others appreciate or benefit from.

It may result in high-intensity creative behaviour that produces a low-benefit creative product, like including cockroaches in each box of soap powder, or Tarquin Vesuvius's self-portrait, or Vincent van Gogh's paintings when the paint was still wet.

I might value the product of my high-intensity creative behaviour, but others might find it an abomination, an insult to the customs, traditions and established mores of the domain and the culture.

FREE - THINKING.

People immersed in a lifetime of accrued conventions can be constricted by them. Knowledge of conventions can be a deterrent to new thinking and creative behaviour. Therefore, the ability to think freely and play with different ideas can be very useful when exploring the unknown.

By not observing the conventions of the domain, I am likely to produce some obvious, weird, dangerous and naïve solutions. But I might also stumble across an amazing, fresh observation that has been missed by someone marinated in the status quo.

Free-thinking gives me liberty to travel deep into the darkness of the unknown and return with something never seen before.

But it may also cause me to stumble and fall.

****

This is why young children are often recognised as being creative, they have few conventions to hinder their creativity. Young children experience everything with new senses.

New-born babies move from a state of creative absurdity towards sensible maturity by learning social conventions. It is only later in life, after they have had communal compliance instilled in them, and they have adopted the existing conventions, their creativity falters.

Older children spend their time desperately trying to learn the community conventions [we are frantically trying to teach them] so they become like the rest of us – good and trustworthy members of the community.

They become sensible, mature, safe, convention obeying .... uncreative. Just like the grown-ups....

"Every child is an artist. The problem is how to remain an artist once we grow up."

Pablo Picasso

We are all born clasping the state of supreme individualism, with only the chemical and biological conventions of the species to sustain us, free from all the rectitude and mewling good manners of civilisation. As we mature, we ascend towards a state of absolute communal absorption, where our individuality – everything we do and think – is obscured beneath the thick, blanket of collective convention.

When we are being creative, we reconnect with the freedom of the pristine individual and the untainted thought of the young child. In that connection, we temporarily throw off the corruption of the status quo and good sense of the moderated majority. In this nest of conceptual vipers, our reality, our behaviour, and our lives, are constructed.... and constricted.

PLAYFULNESS.

If we become aware of the conventions that limit us, we can practice the discipline of ignoring, forgetting or temporarily suspending them. We can practice identifying our containing conventions and learn to play with them. This is one of the skills of creative behaviour.

Some people find this easy. Some require time and effort, but we can all do it – if we try. We can all rediscover a state of creative innocence, a return to a time before we thought we knew all the answers. We can allow ourselves to play with the unknown and revisit the fresh, unconventional insight of the young child.

CONFIDENCE.

Perhaps confidence would help my creative travels. Confidence can be linked with knowledge, but sometimes it comes with naiveté and bravado. Creative confidence is the belief we are capable of finding a solution, out there in the darkness. Such certainty is often found in the young, but also in the 'too old to care' attitude of the mature. A belief that there is a solution is a fundamental part of creative behaviour. If we do not believe there is a solution, we will give up quickly without a struggle. We will scurry back to the circle of conventions and agree with our friends about the futility of trying. We will wear the badge, fold our arms, and employ traditional excuses that justify our inability. A belief there is an answer to the problem – that there is hope in the darkness – sustains and drives creativity. Sometimes this belief can appear to be irrational, illogical, even dangerous – often it is unfulfilled – but it is a volatile driver of creative behaviour.

PRACTICE.

We need to enjoy the process of being creative and not be intimidated by the dark. We need to be able to welcome the challenge of the problem and revel in the excitement of exploring the unknown.

Many people shy away from creative behaviour because it can be frightening. We cannot be sure what we might find in the darkness. Consequently, learning to enjoy the process of being lost, and finding our own way home, is a very important skill that needs to be practiced and learnt.

UNBLOCKING.

When being creative, indifference to the societal mores, even a rejection of the community, is a useful attribute. If we are too conscious of the opinions of others, if we are too concerned with our social standing, or worried about making a fool of ourselves, we will not risk exhibiting our innermost thoughts and feelings to criticism. It is far safer to let others get involved in risky creative behaviour. It is far safer to applaud, boo from the stalls, and laugh at the critic's unflattering comments.

If we are to be creative, we need to accept we may appear different. We need to admit we might stand out from the crowd, and upset people. Sometimes we can appear and, very often, be stupid.

If we are too respectful of the status quo we will not challenge the conventions of those we have been taught to respect. If we do not disconnect from these authority figures, we shall always be trying to please them. We shall always be trying to conform to the conventions they have instilled in us.

We will behave in a way our benefactors like – so we can receive their applause, their commission, their respect, their money, their good grades, their friendship, their acceptance.

179

The range of people that influence us will vary with each individual and each domain: close family, partners, work colleagues, bosses, teachers, peers, religious leaders, our customers or patrons, past champions of the domain. Searching out these figures in our lives, questioning their value, and deliberately breaking their hold on our creative behaviour, is an important step in allowing ourselves to step across the circumference, so we can move into our own unique creativity zone. If we are to be creative, these are the conversations we need to have.

****

This is one of the many problems of the teacher – particularly teachers of arts subjects. The teacher needs to advise, instruct and teach – but to do so without turning the student into a convention craving clone. This is virtually impossible with traditional teaching systems. The student inevitably learns to respond to the teacher's praise, and to scour for any signs of displeasure or disapproval.

Traditionally, the student learns to sate the teacher's ego, so the test can be passed and the quota of exam passes is filled. So the politician can point to percentages and statistics – and take credit for improving 'the system'. But in reality, they are just shovelling more dirt into the broken barrow.

SELF- AWARENESS.

It is not just other people that stand in our way. Often, ***we***, with our hard-set conventions, are the biggest obstacle.

Sometimes we have to analyse our thoughts, so we can examine what is blocking our actions and our ability to be creative. Then we need to remove that block, so our creativity can function properly.

Many of our oldest conventions block creativity: fear of failure, self-doubt, negative thoughts and obstructive feelings. Plus, those influences which were instilled in us when very young. All these conspire with the fast-setting conventions of the moment.

Undoubtedly, the most formidable personal blocks are those taught by parents and close family: those lessons that taught us right and wrong, those lessons that make up our characters, personalities and values, and which affect a thousand different domains. By complying with these blocks, we do what others have instilled in us, we reinforce other people's conventions. We become absorbed into the community, we adopt the uniform: our individuality is smothered and diluted.

Sometimes the safest place is the jail.

It is this oscillating tension between the individual and the community which shapes our lives and our behaviours.

It is at this point – when we identify and dismantle our blocks – that supreme creative behaviour often happens.

When splashing and choking in the unknown. When trying to hold our heads above the crashing waves. When grasping for straws in the tide of convention. When trying to avoid drowning in the comforting syrup of communal rectitude. When fighting to kick off the concrete boots of the status quo.

BOUNDARY BREAKER.

Many that try to behave creatively describe the necessity of finding the boundaries in their lives, so they can cross them.

They search for that moment in their behaviour when they feel they are being repelled, a feeling they are in the wrong territory: the uncomfortable feeling that comes with venturing outside of their circle of conventions.

Once they find this point, they investigate the thought, or feeling, through their work. They purposely set out to destroy their own, most solid, conventions. In this way, they become familiar with creative behaviour, crossing the circumference, and exploring the unknown.

The circumference of our circle of conventions becomes another depiction of the mental block.

By crossing over the line, by moving beyond the walls, the person attempting to solve their problem finds something that is personal and unique.

This explains the sometimes idiosyncratic and challenging work that is the characteristic of the 'avant-garde' in many domains.

****

It is tempting to think we must stop constructing these blocks in our minds, and in the minds of our children. But that may be too extreme: sometimes we need these blocks, so we can function in the status quo. These walls are often there to protect us – as well as contain us.

What we need to do is to become aware of these obstacles, and learn how we can examine, question and analyse them.

The ability to remove, climb, ignore or walk around the walls of our containment, is a most valuable characteristic when exploring our creativity.

When investigating our limits, we do not need to be destructive: we can explore our blocks just by becoming conscious of them, by exposing them, writing about them, or talking about them; then we may decide whether they are worth dismantling – or building upon

Alternatively, we could accept them as the edges of our unique world–part of what makes us different.

Just because there are boundaries does not mean they should be broken. Sometimes, there are very good reasons for their existence. Sometimes, we should raise a flag on these frontiers. Sometimes, we should build a castle and defend them.

We can work within our borders – or drill holes in them, set windows in them, build shelters from them, dance on them.

Whatever we decide to do, we need to discover what our allotted limitations look like – and how they got there.

We do not need to be creative all the time.

After all, we do not want to be like Tarquin Vesuvius!

Or maybe we do...... Who am I to construct such an untimely block?

PATIENCE.

In the search for a solution, I have to be patient. Often finding the right creative product takes time. There are no rules that govern the amount of time and effort a person should take over searching for the right answer. Sometimes, I have to return to the circle of conventions to think through and explore a hybrid idea. Sometimes, I need to spend time moving between conventions and creativity. And, of course, sometimes the creative behaviour fails, no matter how much time and effort are spent looking for a solution.

****

All of the above qualities are important to the person that wants to be creative, but they will not appear equally to each person. Some people may have qualities that are surplus to requirements, and some of them may be more developed. Some of these qualities may be deficient, and some may be ephemeral. Some qualities may only be present in certain environments; some may need developing through training, practice or experience.

The presence of some of these qualities, will depend upon the nature of the domain. Sometimes, creativity will only be possible when all these qualities are present and aligned. Sometimes, creativity will falter when just one of these qualities is absent or skewed. This cocktail of qualities makes for the varying nature of creative behaviour. The variability of these factors, in one person, accounts for reports of the slippery and fluid character of creativity.

As we have seen elsewhere, many people will only feel confident being creative in one domain. These people often have great knowledge of the conventions of a particular subject. This allows them to stand astride the circumference, to fiddle and improve existing solutions, producing low-intensity, but very popular and beneficial creative products.

Some people do not have enough determination, or are too worried about the impact of creativity on their lives. Consequently, their work may be limited, and not reach its potential.

Some people may lack the confidence to pursue a solution to a satisfactory conclusion. Some may wish to be very creative, but have their creativity restricted by the influence of an authority figure, or some other block. Consequently, they rein in their most interesting creativity, to avoid shocking or alienating others.

****

Perhaps the most interesting observation about these characteristics of creative behaviours is that they can be re-classified with negative connotations. Members of the community will often apply adverse interpretations to these qualities. Some may cast self-confidence as arrogance or conceit. We might re-form knowledge of conventions as cleverness, nerdiness or superior behaviour. Dogged determination can be taken as bloody-mindedness, not knowing when to give up, or stubbornness.

The ability to forget our conventions, and return to a childlike way of looking at the world, is often presented as immaturity, irresponsibility or self-indulgence.

By casting a negative light on these creative qualities, the community attempts to restrict the individual in their struggle with their unsolved problems, and in their journeys outside of the circle of conventions. The community supplies the blocks to free-thinking and creative problem solving.

These recalibrations of creative qualities, into anti-social traits, are attempts to make the individual conform to the traditional behaviours of the community. They are an effort to balance the tensions between the risky creativity of the individual and the safe conventions of the group.

If we can identify and speak openly about our creativity blocks, we can understand them, become familiar with them, and reduce their restrictive power.

In addition, we can help critics to recognise the damage their negative comments and attitudes can have. We could agree to stop suppressing those that are trying to be creative. Furthermore, we can nurture and start to applaud their struggle with their unknown.

3.6. THE ESSENTIAL PROBLEM.

Many qualities may aid my journey into the creativity zone: some of them may be necessary, some of them may be useful, some of them may be complementary.

But there is one thing that is vital. If it were missing, I would not stand a chance of being creative.

Without an unsolved problem, big enough to force me outside of my circle of conventions, against my most logical fears, I will not stray into the creativity zone. I will stay at home and enjoy all the benefits of a safe, contented, happy status quo. I will use tried and tested conventions to solve all my problems.

I may possess the highest levels of the creative attributes seen in the last chapter, but if I am not troubled by a problem that is essential to solve – if I have no complaints about the status quo – then these creative qualities will have nothing to work on.

If I do not recognize a problem as important – if some aspect of my life does not irk me – I will find other ways to spend my time. I will follow the recipe. I shall paint by numbers. I shall write in the style others have sanctioned. I shall keep to the script. I will sing someone else's song.

In this way, the lack of creativity becomes a vote for the status quo and the existing conventions.

But, of course, this is what most of us do... most of the time.

The highest intensity creative behaviour often comes from those most bothered by the way things are, those people not satisfied by the existing convention. These are the people that ask the most interesting questions.

If the problem is big enough all the creative qualities can be aroused. As long as we are challenged by a problem that cannot be solved by using conventions we will be driven to some level of creative behaviour. The unsolved problem drives creativity – in all domains. If the problem is common to all of us, the solution will be important to all of us. And the resulting creative product will undoubtedly become a high-benefit creative product.

If the problem only affects a few people, the creative behaviour will produce a low-benefit creative product.

If the creative behaviour causes problems for others, we can identify some level of malcreativity in the solution.

If the creative behaviour solves a small problem in a large composition, this is an example of small creativity.

If the solution only solves a problem for a short amount of time, we can consider it an example of ephemeral creativity.

If the solution is found easily, we can say it has used low-intensity creative behaviour.

If finding the solution takes lots of effort and time, we can say it has used high-intensity creative behaviour.

We are all capable of creativity. We are all capable of exploring the unknown; all we need is a problem that cannot be solved by using conventions.

The recognition of our unsolved problems is the most important part of the creativity equation. If we do not recognise our problems, we do not create new solutions – we do not learn, we do not grow and we do not evolve.

It is the seething malcontent with the status quo that drives our creativity ever onwards, in an attempt to explore the dissonance between our problems and our conventions.

Every new solution pushes out the circumference of the circle of conventions. In that process, we reveal more of the hidden environment that we live in.

But we should be careful;

in the words of Albert Einstein:

'As the circle of the light of knowledge expands, so does the circumference of darkness surrounding it.'

3.7. THE CREATIVE PRODUCT.

Now we can further familiarise ourselves with the properties and qualities of the creative product, and its relationship with what we have learnt so far. I shall do that by extending the story of my itchy snitch.

After spending an enormous amount of time deep in the creativity zone, I have developed a creative product that solves my problem. It's a skin cream that stops my nose itching.

Now, I can stop behaving creatively and return to 'normal'. I can return to the safety and contentment of the circle of conventions. This skin cream is the creative product, the result of my hard work, the consequence of my creative behaviour.

The pot of cream that solved the problem of my sickly snout, consumed a lot of my time, effort and thought. I spent many months exploring the darkness of the unknown, looking for new combinations of materials and compounds, playing with ingredients, juggling with ideas.

Eventually, after extensive trial and error, I found a combination of ingredients that worked. I rubbed the preparation onto my itchy snitch four times a day with a goose feather. After three days the itching stopped. I had found the solution to my problem!

The brew is an old Romany remedy for goat scab, coupled with an Ancient Egyptian potion used to alleviate rashes caused by the chemicals used for mummifying cats.

I have put the mixture into an old jam jar. Because of its illustrious lineage, I am going to call the ointment, 'The Pharaoh's Itch Cream'.

[Of course, none of this is true. I have invented this story to complement the made-up problem of the itchy nose, and to provide us with an example of a creative product.]

Now my creative behaviour is over. I do not need to go back to the darkness of the creativity zone. I have the answer to my problem: the creative product.

The creative product can take many forms. A common conception is the physical object: the sculpture, the poem, a new formula, a new invention... a new itch remedy.

But the creative product can inhabit more than the material world: it can affect our ideas, our behaviours, our thoughts, our beliefs, the words we speak, the movements we make.

Primarily, the creative product changes our minds. The newly conceived creative product is founded upon fresh neural pathways in the maker's head. These fresh neural pathways are the blueprint, or conceptual foundations, for any physical creative product that might be created outside of the maker's mind.

Whatever physical form the creative product might take, it should be noted there is no creative behaviour in the creative product, just as there is no person in the portrait, meal in the recipe, or holiday in the postcard.

The creative product is the result of the ideas and insights discovered or invented through creative behaviour – by exploring the unknown.

At the point of completion, the creative product is only of benefit to the person that created it. Therefore, it always begins its journey as an extreme low-benefit creative product.

Once the creative product has been brought into existence, it can be exhibited to the community. From here, other people can assess it, talk about it, copy it. If appropriate, it can be adopted by others, and used to solve their own problems.

But it may not last long in this form. If it solves many other people's problems, the low-benefit creative product will be transformed into something much more powerful and rare: the high-benefit creative product.

3.8. THE HIGH BENEFIT CREATIVE PRODUCT.

Now we can follow the progress of 'The Pharaoh's Itch Cream' as it turns from an unknown, low-benefit creative product; into a world-changing, high-benefit creative product.

Now I have the solution to my problem, I can leave the turbulence of the creativity zone, and return to the comfort of a 'normal' life in the circle of conventions. I can go back to the safety of my community.

Here, I feel a palpable relief from the stresses and strains of being creative. I have improved my life. I feel happy. At last, I can bathe in the glory of my success. I can put my feet up, light a pipe or two – even throw a party.

The creative behaviour is over; the problem has been solved: my itch has gone.

When I am back inside the circle of conventions, I place the pot of cream just inside the circumference of the circle. Now, the community can take a closer look at my creation and learn from my experiences.

I am not the sort of person that seeks out the limelight. I have no particular desire to show off my creative product to anyone else, but I have to confess, my relief and happiness has driven a desire to celebrate the end of my problem.

I have a feeling of elation which makes the whole world seem more comfortable. This euphoria tempts me to cast aside my natural introversion, and show-off the product of my creative behaviour.

Furthermore, other people in my community want to shove me centre stage. They have been worried about me. They are badgering me for information about my nose. They all tried to help with my problem; now they are interested to see how it has been solved.

For a while, I was a figure of much communal fun and gossip. Now that the community has seen that my problem has been cured, a similar process starts. Only this time they are all interested in how I found a remedy. Now the chatter is about my perfectly cured snout.

"How did I solve the problem?"

"What did I do to stop the itch?"

"How long did it take?"

Subconsciously, they have all been worried about what would happen if they suffered an itch like mine.

Because we are all similar, an unsolved problem for one member of the community is an unsolved problem for everyone; consequently, they all want to know the details of my journey into the creativity zone. Such a newsworthy and interesting creative product could be the subject of talk and gossip for many months to come.

In these circumstances, it would be difficult to stop the news spreading. The number of people aware of my problem is extensive. The driver of the inquisition is their anxiety.

Everyone is trying to make their lives better. If they can learn about the new product, it may also improve their lives. They might go to bed tonight feeling a little happier.

They might feel a little more secure: not so anxious about their itchy elbows, or the dry skin on their son's knee. If this cream works, the community, and by extension the species, will have pushed back the boundary of the unknown.

I will have shone a light into our communal darkness.

In real life – away from my deliberations about creativity – placing a low-benefit creative product inside the circumference of our group circle of conventions, and exposing it to the community, can be a metaphor for many types of publicity.

Depending upon the nature of the product, I could advertise it in the papers, tell my friends about it, wear it to pick up the kids from school, hold an exhibition, go on tour, put it on the internet, publish it, or spread the good news by word of mouth.

As a species, we have developed many commercial and social structures to celebrate newsworthy creative products.

As soon as I display the cream, the rest of the community is interested. Straight away, Uncle Derek asks if he can try it. Apparently, he has a similar itch. Uncle Derek's itch has been causing problems, on and off, for years.

Two days later, Uncle Derek returns in jubilation: it has cured his itch too!

Significantly, when Uncle Derek solves his problem, he also becomes a transmitter of the good news. Now, even more people are aware of the problem-solving qualities of the cream.

When I first created my nose itch cure, it was an extreme low-benefit creative product, only of interest and benefit to myself, but when other people use it, and find it useful, it starts to move towards the middle– and then to the high-benefit end– of the spectrum.

Each time someone uses the cream– and benefits from its use – the more the nose cream grows in cultural influence and reliability. Over time, with repeated use, my creative product becomes a full-blooded cultural monster, found in every home, used by royalty, commoners; stars of stage and screen.

Now, it has become the first choice for all skin ailments. Doctors prescribe 'The Pharaoh's Itch Cream' for their patients. They neatly forget their initial scoffing, and scathing criticisms, of my attempts to find a cure.

Soon, if the creative product continues to solve problems, thousands, maybe millions of people, will benefit from it.

With the machinations of communication networks, we do not have to be a creative problem solver to make our lives better: we just need to know one, read about one, listen to the gossip about one – or be the member of the same species as one.

Today the world is populated by billions of people, all striving to make their lives better, by solving their individual problems.

With the use of the internet, and new communication technologies, news of a new creative product can spread around the globe faster than the world can spin. Eventually, the whole world can benefit from my creativity.

But only if it solves a problem.

If the creative product does not solve a problem for others, it will hold no importance for anyone else; it will not be copied or passed on. The amount of time and effort that went into finding the creative product – the intensity of the creative behaviour – will be irrelevant; the main value of the creative product is as a problem solver.

Furthermore, it is only culturally **successful,** and considered to be a high-benefit creative product, if it solves many people's problems, and many people adopt it.

This is the same for my itch cream as it is for an improved recipe, a new scientific breakthrough, or an innovative design, a new painting, a new novel.

As it is, my itch cream is well on the way to becoming a cultural icon, bought and stored in everybody's medicine cabinet – indispensable to all.

What started as an answer to my itchy problem, concocted from my fumbling chemical experiments, in my spare bedroom, will be converted into something that has the ability to last forever.

In the future, creative products may be used to transport our descendants across the universe. Alternatively, they could – in the form of a malcreative product – blow us all to dust.

In the realm of ideas – in the empire of the non-material and the transient – the creative product is a communication, capable of infiltrating our heads and changing our behaviours.

Whenever we use a creative product, we support and strengthen the message it contains. We become transmitters of that message. We enable it, even recommend it, to be passed on to others.

In this way, our community reality, our status quo, is composed of the problems that our cultures have identified and chosen to solve in the past with creativity.

****

And now we can observe the most spectacular transformation of the new creative product. The high-benefit creative product – day by day, year by year – converts from a weird, untried, risky proposition, into a dull, trustworthy, dependable and boring convention: something that is tried, tested and trusted by all.

In the guise of a convention, the former creative product has the ability to exist for millennia, solving problems, changing lives, making people safer and happier travelling across continents, from culture to culture, lasting well beyond the transitory brain, blood and bones and creative behaviour of the maker.

In this way, the one-time creative product can pass through the generations: as an activity, a tool, a recipe, a belief, an image or idea; most importantly, in the altered neural pathways and behaviours we first conceived on the African grassland – even in the life changing choices we made as that curious primate in our evolutionary infancy.

Our modern day lives are a back-catalogue of the creative products our species has chosen to turn into conventions over millions of years, in response to the constant assault of the ever-changing environment. Our history is the history of our creativity.

****

But that it does not end there.

We now need to examine the vital process that is responsible for making this cataclysmic transmutation.

This process is essential to our understanding of the relationship between creative products, problem-solving and conventions.

And it explains many of the anomalies that have dogged the understanding of creativity through the ages.

That process is called the law of diminishing returns.

3.9. *THE LAW OF DIMINISHING RETURNS.*

When I first discovered the solution to my nose itch, I was beside myself with elation. I could not believe I had found a solution. I danced in the street. I shouted "Eureka!" The new skin cream is seen, by all, as a miraculous breakthrough, a marvel of modern medicine, and my creativity.

As it transforms, from a high-benefit creative product into a convention, 'The Pharoah's Itch Cream' becomes absorbed into the culture of the community: it is drawn inwards, moving closer to the centre of the convention circle.

At the same time, my exhilaration diminishes. By the twentieth use of the cream there was hardly any excitement at all. By the fiftieth use my joy at finding a solution disappears completely.

Over many years, my astounding high-benefit creative product becomes just another dull convention – just another workaday solution to a simple problem. Worse than this: eventually, I look at the pot and feel boredom. That burning racing excitement I initially felt – that exhilaration that kept me awake when I first discovered the cream – has turned into turgid plasma congealing tedium. Now, the Pharoah's Itch Cream is just another conventional preparation in my groaning bathroom cabinet. The same happens in the wider world.

When the community first experienced the new skin cream, they also got excited, but with each exposure the convention becomes part of the status quo and their enthusiasm fades.

This transformation, from an exciting, rousing creative product, into a boring convention, is the law of diminishing returns at work.

We need to appreciate this process.

****

When we first solve a problem, an expectation is created: our lives are going to get better. Our brains focus on the new solution, and it forms fresh neural pathways to accommodate it. However, with repeated exposure the excitement diminishes, our senses become accustomed to the stimuli.

With repeated use, the creative product slowly becomes transformed into a convention, and an accepted part of 'the way things are'.

Each time we hear the hilarious joke, the laughter decreases.

Each time we see the outrageous film, the shock wanes.

Each time we use the new invention, the wonder subsides.

Slowly, with each use, the initial exhilaration dissipates.

Then it disappears altogether, as the high-benefit creative product becomes a well-used, trusted, reliable convention – part of our stable culture.

This is how once scandalous artworks become decorations on biscuit tins. This is how books that once topped the bestseller list now languish in the bargain basket. This is how clothes that once needed a mortgage to buy are found in the charity shop.

This is why we can never really appreciate the exhilaration a newly-conceived creative product held when it was first unleashed upon the world.

Try to imagine the cataclysmic elation when Mankind first beat a drum, grew wheat, lit a fire, weaved, painted a bison, or tasted chocolate. It is impossible. Those astounding creative products changed those people, and all that followed them.

After many years of use, the Pharoah's Itch Cream still solves problems, but the problem has been diminished; it has become easy to solve. The problem is no longer irritating, or seen as difficult: the problem has a common, conventional solution. Everyone has the answer; it is no longer a worry.

The original adrenaline inducing creative product eventually prompts boredom. Because we know there is an easy solution on the shelf, nobody worries about getting an itch. Everyone feels better. Everyone *is* better.

In this way, our children are born into the world our ancestors transformed, improved and refined. Our world is the creative product of all those people before us that strived for survival.

We are all dependent on this huge accumulation of creative behaviour. It started at the first drops of life: with the seed of the evolutionary tree. The collective minds of our ancestors ventured deep into their dark unknown, and returned with the most astounding and vital creative products. It is those creative products we rely upon today as our most trusted conventions.

Today, my fourteen-month-old granddaughter is able to press enough buttons on her mother's phone to make the music play. Olivia, can use technology that a few years ago only existed in the frenzied mind of a science fiction writer, and she can use it before she can form a sentence or feed herself.

In this way, today's creativity is forming our unborn children's environments, minds and lives, just as the creativity and problems of the past has formed ours. Creative product, by creative product, our species is fulfilling its most ancient desires. We are becoming what we have always destined to be....

Our species hurtles through time and space, propelled by our creativity. As yet, we have not asked the question – where to? Where is our creativity taking us? If our creativity is making our world, what sort of world is it to be? And, more importantly, what sort of world should it be? If our creativity makes us what we are, what is our creativity doing to us? What is our destiny?

In the past, one person's creative behaviour had the power to inflate the circle of conventions to improve the world. Today, for the first time in history, one person can just as easily destroy it with one malcreative act. In our eternal quest for divine power, in our constant search for absolute control, Mankind has created a dangerous and fragile world. With each creative solution, the circumference of our circle of convention expands, becoming thinner and more delicate. With each new solution, we expose many new problems. How long before we are unable to solve one of those problems with creativity? How long before one of those problems causes our circle to burst?

THE FINAL SOLUTION.

We cannot know the future,

but I fear, with many others,

that our creativity,

which till now has facilitated and propelled our species,

will turn on us,

and become the thing that destroys us.

Until we recognise the problem

we shall not be able to solve it.

The problem that has accompanied us,

in the next carriage down,

all the way through this amazing journey:

how do we stop using our creativity to destroy?

Eventually, it will blow us all back to dust,

returning us to inanimate harmony once more:

dark dust, ash and indolent chemicals,

spinning through the stratosphere,

trying to find balance in an inherently unstable Universe –

settling at the bottom of the toxic oceans,

to begin again....in a final solution.

kjb.

3.10. OTHER PRESENTATIONS OF CREATIVITY.

We have used the story of the Pharoah's Itch Cream to track and explore the trajectory of the high-benefit creative product, and seen how it turns into a convention. Also, we have illustrated the role the law of diminishing returns plays in the process. Now we can apply this method to some of the other less traditional presentations of creativity.

What process occurs when the creative product fails to benefit lots of people?

****

On my return from the creativity zone, flushed with success, and very pleased with my work, I bring my itch cure concoction into the community convention circle. Immediately, people rush around to see the new product. They want to see how I solved my problem. They pick up the jar and smell the contents. They read the label. They rub the cream on their hands. However, in this case, it does not benefit anyone else. Nobody has the same itch as me. Therefore, they have no need for a new itch cream. Consequently, the creative product remains ignored, unvalued and must be considered of low-benefit.

My itch cream may be the result of months of high-intensity creative behaviour, but if it does not solve other people's problems it will have little benefit or value to the community.

In addition, the constant smearing of my nose with this smelly, sticky substance leads some people to consider me a little bit strange, weird, eccentric – even mad. A creative product that does not benefit other people will often be viewed as an affront to the rest of society, and their hard-earned conventions. This is the fate of many, very interesting, low-benefit creative products and many people that have behaved creatively.

BRIEFED CREATIVITY.

What social processes accompany briefed creativity? In this example, the itchy nose belongs to someone else – commonly known as the client.

On behalf of the client, I take a trip into the creativity zone in an effort to find a solution to their itchy nose. Traditionally, a brief is created that details the parameters of the work and the result the client requires.

In our new understanding we can see that this sort of problem is an external and objective problem, located nearer the scientific end of the external/internal spectrum of problems.

This type of problem is easier to identify, discuss and transpose into a brief than the internal subjective problem.

"I want a cream that cures my itchy nose. I want it by the end of the month, and I will pay you three hundred and fifty pounds."

I duly go about my work, employing creative behaviour to solve the client's problem. After months of intense creative behaviour, I show the client what I have created for them.

Two days after delivery, the client's nose problem is cured. Naturally, the client is ecstatic with the result of my labour. So, the client pays the agreed fee; the brief has been successfully completed. The scientific/external creative product is usually assessed upon its function, using strict objective criteria.

However, writing a brief for an internal problem, that emanates from a person's mind, would not be so straight forward. The successful solution, to an internal problem, is often subjective which makes it hard to transpose into words. Traditionally, this sort of personal problem would be solved through one of the artistic domains.

In short, you cannot expect someone else to solve an artistic problem. You cannot get someone else to write your poem for you, paint for you, or play your music for you, and expect the resulting creative product to succeed in solving your particular subjective artistic problem.

Traditionally, artistic creative product are solutions to problems that comes from the mind of the unique individual. It is difficult to describe what the final artwork should look using words. Imagine writing a brief for *Da Vinci's* Mona Lisa, or *Rodin's* the Kiss; you could fill an encyclopaedia with the makers requirements.

This would be the same for any visual artwork. The artistic/internal creative product is usually assessed using subjective criteria, which cannot be proven, as they are they are opinions.

Often, people that work in artistic domains do not recognise a definable problem, they just feel an internal dissatisfaction. It is this dissatisfaction with their status quo that drives them to explore their unknown, and produce, often very personal, artworks.

Often artists will hunt around in the dark of the creativity zone, unsure of what they are looking for. The internal problem is the foundation of the artistic domains.

This, I think, is the difference between Art and Design.

If a problem can be reduced to a brief, and the success of that brief can be objectively assessed, then the embryonic creative product is most likely to be a piece of design.

However, if the problem and its solution cannot be reduced to the words of a brief, then the creative product is probably a piece of art. Generally, the nascent work of art is too personal to be communicated to someone else. It is only possible to achieve an agreeable solution to the problem through the medium of the artistic domain. And, most importantly, it is only possible for the person with the problem [the artist] to solve the problem.

Of course, this is not a firm or definite division: much design crosses over to the arts, and much art affects design – hence the term 'Art and Design'.

However, the division is worth erecting, and maintaining, as a soft and permeable fence between the two domains, and as an aid to our understanding.

EPHEMERAL CREATIVITY.

Some creative products only solve our problems for a short period of time. In this example, thousands of people use the nose cream and marvel at its problem-solving abilities. However, in a few months a better skin product replaces it, or it is found the problem is just as easily solved by using a conventional concoction. In which case, my nose cream quickly stops being a high-benefit creative product and passes into the annals of social history as a fad, a fashion, a passing phase. Just like the hula-hoop, the ruff, the 'twist' or the top hat.

An ephemeral creative product catches the community's imagination – solves their problem for a few moments – then disappears. The unrestrained output of ephemeral creative products feeds our lust for novelty and entertainment. Each ephemeral creative product struggles against the indomitable law of diminishing returns.

SMALL CREATIVITY.

Earlier in the book, I described small creativity as something that was unwittingly obscured in larger complex creative products. For this example, I shall use a slightly different expression.

In this case, we need to imagine the Pharaoh's Itch Cream as a conventional medicinal preparation which has been solving problems for decades. Using small creativity, I will attempt to improve the product by making minor changes to the older, well-established convention.

I am going to add a new component to the old concoction that changes its natural colour, then I will give it a new perfume: *'Sunrise over the Nile'*.

Once it is exhibited in the circle of convention, the crowds flock to try the new 'improved' formula. The community is obliged, by their natural curiosity, to investigate. This sort of small creativity is constantly used in commerce and business to engender new interest in a solid convention that has become battered by the law of diminishing returns.

Small creativity is a very popular form of creativity. The reasons for this are clear. First, small creativity is easier to produce. I do not have to spend months in the creativity zone, searching for a completely new solution to an entirely new problem. All I have to do is find a tired convention. Then I stand on the circumference, tinker around in the unknown, and find an improvement that makes the existing solution slightly better.

The second reason this form of creativity is popular, is it is less risky. I do not have go through the abundant 'errors and terrors' that accompany larger expressions of creativity. All I have do is tweak the convention a little, rejuvenate it, and make it appear new again.

The community receives a small nudge, accompanied by a hug of comforting novelty. Consequently, the masses find it much easier to understand the small creativity: it is much easier to digest the creativity pill when it is hidden in a feast of convention.

Big, complex creative products can be scary, difficult to understand and assimilate; they challenge long-held community conventions. Gargantuan ideas like evolution, 3-D films, Cubism, and atheism take time to become accepted. These are not nudges, but great big cultural shoulder charges that can knock you off your feet.

By adopting small creative products, we make slight changes to our lives; however, because of the ubiquity of the small creative product – because of their universal application – they are often hard to recognise.

The small creative product is often hidden in our everyday behaviours. Often it can be so small it occurs inside our heads without us realising it: we might drop a word from our vocabulary, reassess an idea, learn how to sew, or stop using salt in our recipes.

In this way, small creative products can accumulate, slowly changing our personalities, our characters, philosophies and values, and of course our lives.

MALCREATIVITY.

So how does a seemingly innocuous, skin preparation become perceived as a piece of malcreativity? In this case, I deposit my creation just inside the circumference of the circle of conventions. Once again, the community comes to investigate, but this time the creative product is met with revulsion.

Perhaps it is the idea that geese are being killed for their feathers. Maybe people are annoyed beeswax is being used, ruining the traditional wax polish industry, or 'factor X' is being imported from a country with a despotic regime. Whatever the reason, enough individuals are caused a problem by my creative product that they are repelled by it. It becomes a repugnant creative product: a piece of malcreativity.

Again, we must remember the creative product, and the level of creative behaviour used in its creation, has not changed. The intrinsic process and ingredients that created the product are exactly the same; it is just the community's perception of the creative product that has altered.

Earlier, I described malcreative products as creativity applied to bad things, like torture chambers, weapons or concentrations camps – these are obvious examples of malcreativity. But, if we tried hard enough, we could find malcreativity in any creative product. Much of the time, what constitutes malcreativity depends on your point of view.

For some, chewing gum can be offensive, for others, comic books – and what about musicals, pop art, high heels, cigarettes or soap operas?

Is the use of expletives malcreative? Is sex and violence acceptable in a film or novel? If so, at what point does it become offensive and unacceptable? Malcreativity can be located on a spectrum that includes naughty pop music lyrics, risqué poetry, pornographic cardigans; all the way to political parties that incite, and reflect, all sorts of offensive ideas and behaviours.

Furthermore, our malcreativity antennae can be sensitive in some domain but not in others. Some people are offended by naughty postcards but not by more extreme graphic images. Whatever the level of perceived offence, it has to be admitted that there will always be some people that consider the product to be beneficial– if it solves their problems. Some find it easy to ignore or disregard the offensive parts of the creative product.

Malcreativity is a permanent feature of our behaviour and our communities. One person's immorality can be another person 'living on the edge'. Some people enjoy the thrill of engaging in 'immoral activities.

Malcreativity exposes our anti-social thoughts and problems. It challenges the rest of us to think about them, copy them, adapt them or reject them. If the malcreative product survives initial censorship, the law of diminishing returns may take effect.

Then, eventually, we can use the naughty lyrics to advertise soap powder, we teach the once outrageous novel in schools, the community offending art exhibition becomes a cultural landmark, the pornographic cardigan is worn by newsreaders–if only at weekends.

 As long as the malcreative product solves enough people's problem it will persist.

It should be recognised that the taint of immorality can sometimes produce an exciting cocktail of pleasure in the 'naughty' creative product.

Many find this brew irresistible.

217

Challenging and offending the status quo, standing outside of the conventional mainstream, 'sticking two fingers up' at the establishment, can be thrilling to some. This added pleasure can turn a malcreative product into a 'cult' classic.

It is a long-standing convention that if you want a copper-bottomed [sorry] hit in British popular music you need to get it banned by the B.B.C.

FAILED CREATIVITY.

Now we can examine the trajectory of the most common result of creative behaviour: failure. This is the creativity that does not solve the problem, not even for the person that was trying to be creative.

In this example, after working for months in the creativity zone, I have nothing to show for my efforts. I can find no antidote to my adenoidal aggravation: I am still scratching my proboscis.

Dejectedly, I haul myself back over the circumference – into the glaring circle of conventions – to the winnowing gaze of a disappointed community. My creative behaviour has failed to find a solution. However, we must not be too disparaging. I may not have a creative product to show for my efforts – but I have behaved creatively. We cannot ignore the fact that I have spent an enormous amount of time and effort attempting to find a solution. I have been hunting around in the creativity zone: taking the risks, doing the work, picking things up, putting them down, juggling them, combining them, taking them apart and putting them back together again.

Some might say I have used more creative behaviour than the person that has just played about on the circumference, using very low-intensity creative behaviour, to generate a very successful, highly beneficial, creative product.

Some might say I have used more creative behaviour than the person that just tinkered with an existing convention, improving a small part to great effect, in the process making life better for millions of people.

Whatever the outcome, we must admit that failure to find a solution can use extremely high intensities of creative behaviour, and that failure can be an essential part of the process of finding a successful creative product.

This, of course, is why I have found a place for the words 'Attempts and Aims' in the definition: without these two words the definition of creativity would have a very different meaning.

Let us assume, for a moment, I did not include these words in the definition – that the definition read: 'Creativity is a spectrum of behaviour that explores our unknown to learn something new or solve a problem.

The spectrum is still apparent, the problems are still there. But the mistakes, the false starts and the failures, that are an inherent and essential part of creativity, are not accounted for.

Without the words 'Attempts and Aims' in the definition, creativity is firmly located in the end result – in the successful creative product.

The definition would then imply there is no creative behaviour leading up to the solution or learning, only in that blinding flash of insight when the answer reveals itself and the problem is solved. The 'Aha!' or 'Eureka!' moment of genius, is a popular misconception of traditional creativity. But it only tells a small fraction of the story. Attempting and trying and failing can be – and usually is – an essential part of creativity.

When we fumble around in that dark space, trying to find a solution to a problem, we often get lost, we often trip, we often get it wrong. Frequently, this is when we employ our highest levels of creative behaviour: when refining our thoughts, when we are tuning into the problem, when we are asking a question we are not sure of, or proposing a solution that appears to be ridiculous.

This is when we are at our most creative: when we embrace the uncertainty, when we close our eyes and draw what we think we see, when we slip a strange phrase out to see if anyone laughs, when making the pass in the hope someone makes the run to meet it; when we think the unthinkable, or we try to compose the idea that has never been composed before.

Today's most resolute conventions were once indescribable, amorphous feelings. They were just fuming ideas, being torn up and stuck back together again in someone's troubled mind. But it is salutary to note, often that sticky tape did not work and the creative product could not be realised.... the creative behaviour failed to produce a successful creative product.

For every beautiful piece of music there are pillars of silent manuscripts– never to be heard.

For every moon landing there are tons of charred wreckage.

For every lifesaving operation there are hundreds of funerals.

For every successful business there are thousands of bankruptcies.

For every short incisive pithy paragraph there is a loquacious over-written list.

Each failure takes us closer to a solution. Each failure is an attempt to make our lives better. Each failure is creativity at work. Here is the raging battle between the status quo and creativity. In that struggle we have the graphic expression of the way cultures evolve. We build our conventional defences, hoping they will protect us from the future, only to have them bent out of shape by the constant battering of the environment and the law of diminishing returns.

Perhaps now we can understand why creativity is such a misunderstood activity in the classroom. Schools acclaim the learning of conventions as evidence of success. One of the chief functions of education is to venerate the achievements of the past. Consequently, naturally occurring creative behaviour, and its attendant failures, is squeezed out of enthusiastic students. All because the mangled pots, misplaced questions, or exploratory stories did not conform to the conventional requirements of the curriculum, the assessment regime or the examination syllabus.

Creativity has been beaten out of schools by successive generations of well-meaning but misguided educationalists. Too many teachers have succeeded in their profession by eschewing failure and creativity. Consequently, they do not understand creative behaviour. They do not know what it looks like; and they have not been required to teach it.

This is not an argument for abandoning the teaching of conventions. We have to teach conventions: if we do not, we will not be able to use our creativity to improve them. But the teaching of conventions needs to be balanced with the teaching of creativity.

With the teaching of creativity, goes the acceptance, validation and joy of failure as a part of creative learning. The disciplines of creative behaviour, and the acquisitions of conventions, need to be put into context and explained to students. In this way, they may understand the nature of the educational environment that they are involved with. We need to recognise that long standing conventions only have full meaning when viewed with an understanding of the creativity that formed them.

Many teachers implicitly recognise the wrongness of traditional education. Many leave the profession early, or do not join. They have an intuitive distrust of the integral structure. The education system 'feels' wrong to them, as it does to many other people – not least the students.

But we continue to fish for balloons; we continue to try and fly our kites indoors.

3.11. THE QUALITY SPECTRUM OF CREATIVITY.

So far, in our efforts to explore and understand creativity, we have formed and examined many spectrums. Now, we need to form a spectrum that explores the essential quality of creativity and answers the question, what makes one creative product more creative than another creative product?

We have seen that effort and time affects the intensity of creative behaviour. But higher intensity creative behaviour does not promise that the creative product will be more creative.

And we have seen that the number of people that benefit from a creative product is not related to the quality of a creative product: often the creative product, that benefits millions, can be the result of a simple tweak of creativity, to a long-standing convention.

So, here is the problem: if we had two creative products next to each other, how would we decide which is the most creative? What factors would make one creative product more creative than another? If we knew this, we would be a lot closer to understanding the essence of creativity. With this understanding, we would be able to improve our own creative behaviour and find creativity a lot easier to teach and assess.

From this postulation, I suggest we need to form a spectrum that describes the varying concentrations of creativity – a spectrum that spans from the lowest quality of creativity to the highest.

If we had one of those, we could use it to identify, compare and improve creative products. Most importantly, with such a spectrum, we should be able to observe and classify the accumulative characteristics that produce increasingly higher qualities of creativity.

For example, we should be able to identify the attributes that differentiate a level-two creative product from a level-seven creative product. At the very least we should be able to recognize the features of lower quality creativity and higher quality creativity.

Then, once we have identified the characteristics that comprise the quality of a piece of creativity, we may be able to extrapolate from them, and apply them to other problems. In this way, we shall form a better understanding of creativity.

****

So, what domain should I use to explore the quality levels of creativity?

Well, since I am communicating my ideas through this book, it seems sensible that I should create a spectrum in the domain of writing.

To this end, I am going to write ten short statements; each will describe the experience of eating the same small portion of very hot chillies. I shall start with a well-used convention for the first account. Then I shall attempt to apply a little more creativity to each description, so the essential quality of creativity increases and becomes more concentrated.

These ten descriptions shall form a spectrum, with the lowest level of creativity to the left [zero level], and the highest level of creativity to the right [level ten].

Once complete, I shall draw conclusions from the spectrum and the experience.

So, this is my proposal....

In the name of science, I am to secrete myself in the damp, pungent leaf litter of my mind, amongst the etymologists and entomologists.

From my hide, I shall observe the soaring creative process play out above me, in the canopy of my neural jungle. Assuming I survive the experience, I shall report back.

Each of the ten chilli eating descriptions [the creative products] will be accompanied by a commentary, which will loosely evaluate and describe the various thoughts and processes I used in the production of the descriptions [the creative behaviour].

These commentaries will attempt to describe my reflections, my observations, and the experience of 'attempting to be creative'.

This activity should provide insight into the nature and qualities used in the creative behaviour, and provide evidence to justify the position of the description on the creative spectrum.

But before I throw myself headlong into the neural compost, we should consider the nature of the challenge, and be clear what the problem is.

As we have learnt, not all problems are the same. Describing the chilli eating experience is more of an artistic, internal problem rather than an external, scientific problem. I have created the problem because I want to make a spectrum that illuminates and exposes creative behaviour. In which case, we can say the problem emanates from the internal world of my mind.

Because the problem is more internal than real, I have a lot more freedom in the creative behaviour I use. I can be much more experimental in my thoughts and behaviour than I would in a scientific problem: no one is going to die if my descriptions of the chillies are poor quality, or a little 'off'. [But please feel free to disagree, or be offended.]

We should also note, because the problem is internal, the solutions I produce will be subjective. I have no way of proving my descriptions are true. Consequently, the reader may not agree with my submissions.

My reports are my opinions, I cannot prove their validity. The writings will only have value if the reader trusts me and agrees with my findings.

If it were an external problem, I could be more objective. I could assess my findings against agreed scientific criteria. I could show my solutions are correct and effective, using confirming data that proves my conclusions.

We shall begin with a solution that contains no creative elements, as it is completely conventional, and would be easily found within the convention circle of many people.

226

ZERO LEVEL CREATIVITY.

[Inside the circle of convention.]

The chillies taste hot and spicy which causes a burning sensation in the mouth and throat.

This is an adequate description of the experience of eating hot chilli peppers.

If we were to ask one thousand people to describe eating a portion of very hot chillies, I would expect over nine hundred would choose to describe it something like this.

Using this depiction, everyone should understand what to expect when eating these chillies. It communicates the experience clearly. However, it isn't very entertaining or very interesting – it is a wholly conventional description.

Because of this lack of originality, I imagine the reader would consider the writing to be dull, monotonous, safe and boredom inducing – not very engaging – and not creative.

But it is worth noting, once this description may have been the height of creative expression for this type of experience.

Now, after long exposure to the law of diminishing returns, it has become a haggard platitude, used by many.

There is no evidence of creative behaviour in this phrase: it does not explore the unknown, it solves the problem using old solutions that have been adopted from other people. It is a tried and tested convention – otherwise known as a cliché.

If I am to be creative, I need to produce something more interesting that contains new expressions feelings and ideas. I need to expose something that was previously unknown.

But we should not move to the next description until we have recognised the value of that description – 'haggard platitude, used by a large majority' – this reveals an important characteristic of creative behaviour.

Creative behaviour is not the work of the majority, it is the work of the minority; in the extreme, the individual. To be more creative, I have to expose more of my unique unknown individuality and suppress my communal homogeneity.

LEVEL ONE. [Across the circumference.]

The chillies are as hot and spicy as a teaspoon of fresh boiling mustard.

Here we have a simple comparison with things that also taste hot and spicy. The description stretches convention just a bit. So, we can say it is more creative than the zero-level example.

The phrase has not used too much effort or time to compose; therefore, we can say it has used low-intensity creative behaviour. We could probably concoct this description by standing on the circumference of conventions and peering into the darkness.

The image of fresh boiling mustard is an expression that is new to me, so we can describe it as creative – but only just. This description provides us with some insight into creative behaviour: as soon as we start to be creative, we move away from well-worn convention. Consequently, the communication becomes more stimulating, but at the same time more difficult to appreciate.

Plus, we can see that there is an element of learning taking place. Some readers will not understand the reference, and some will have to struggle to create new neural pathways in an attempt to grasp and assimilate the image of 'fresh boiling mustard'.

In that word construction, we are slightly challenged and slightly excited. We have to use our imaginations, and work a little harder, to make a connection.

We are required to 'tune into' the message being transmitted, so we can understand it. In that process we are slightly entertained.

This description bonds thoughts and feelings to words, then uses them to communicate this new experience.

Although others have described eating chillies before, they would not have used this precise form of words, or expressed their thoughts and feelings like this.

The description has inflated our circle of collective experience – just a little – by the unique, and slightly creative, observation.

LEVEL TWO.

If I am going to be more creative, I need to push deeper into the creativity zone, further away from my conventions, to expose something that is a little more inventive.

The chillies taste like a teaspoon of boiling mustard, taken with a shot of twelve-year-old malt whisky.

Here, I have improved upon the previous description, by adding another reference. Mixing the two tastes from disparate sources causes a more complex synthesis of ideas and images. This moves the description deeper into the creativity zone, making the description a more concentrated cocktail.

The whisky reference forces us to imagine the mixture of boiling mustard coupled with twelve-year-old malt whiskey. This is a more difficult union of tastes and ideas to play with, but in terms of the definition of creativity – does it show evidence of exploring the unknown or an attempt to solve a new problem?

Does it make for a more perceptive description; therefore, a better understanding of the experience? I think the answer is yes: if only because the description is longer and adds something new to the previous account.

But assuming the description is accurate, it also reveals something about the taste of chillies that previous attempts did not. Consequently, it conveys a new subjective observation, that makes the communication richer and more informative than previous accounts: something new has been learnt about the taste of the chillies.

LEVEL THREE.

The chillies are as hot as hell in a heat wave, and as spicy as the devil himself.

This is a combination of conventional phrases, assembled to create a new message. *'Hot as hell'* is an unoriginal phrase, but when it is combined with *'in a heat wave'* it pushes the convention a little further along the spectrum. However, this may be an arrangement of words I have heard somewhere before. I may have inadvertently used a convention thinking I am being creative.

This is a common experience. When we try to be creative, we can be influenced by expressions that may be unknown to us but known to other people. In this way, we unconsciously use a 'young' convention as we play just outside the circumference of our own experiences, thinking they are devices we have invented.

In spite of this, there is no doubt that adding the image of 'the devil' provides an interesting and fresh feature. Consequently, this example is slightly more creative than level two, as it refers to experiences beyond the domain of food, or the sense of taste.

This description challenges us to imagine the chilli eating event by using a combination of disparate references, disconnected from taste.

The second part of the description, *'as spicy as the devil himself'*, refers to the devil, which is commonly considered to be a fearful and bad character.

But this image is moderated and softened by using it to describe an inert meal of chillies.

The personification [or demonization] of a taste makes the chilli description even more complex, pushing it further away from my circle of convention. Eating chillies is presented as interesting – like an exciting and dangerous character – like the devil.

The use of alliteration might also convey the sensation of the experience. The gasping 'Haitches' of the account mimic the repeated staccato expulsion of air that can occur when eating something hot.

The monosyllabic words may also symbolise the stepped transition of the taste from tongue, to lips, to stomach. Or it could just make a more interesting sound description than previous offerings.

I am beginning to play with the form in the description.

As I push along the spectrum, the amount and breadth of creativity I use is increasing.

In earlier descriptions, I was playing with small aspects of the convention; now I am making larger incursions as I venture deeper into the unknown.

[Please note: this is the same chilli eating event as described in level zero and one, two and three. It is just the creative behaviour used in the description that has changed.]

LEVEL FOUR.

Eating the chillies is like the devil's angels dancing on my tongue.

This is more creative than previous levels as it has almost completely moved away from the convention of taste. Now the symbols are more remote.

The description infers hot and spicy, but it does not mention these features by name. It alludes to the *'heat of hell'* through the device of the devil's angels. By conflating the angels with a devil, and applying it to the experience of tasting hot chillies, it makes the description more original, new, different and ultimately more entertaining.

I have noticed, that in an attempt to be more creative, I have stopped being so prescriptive and obvious. This description allows the reader to supply their own pictures and conjure their own interpretation.

This makes the report more difficult to interpret, perhaps less precise and more challenging. Consequently, I think it is more thought provoking. The surreal image of *'angels dancing on the tongue'* requires the reader to make a synesthetic connection between taste and dancing, which makes the synaptic jungle fizz.

The description is definitely more stimulating and more entertaining. [In the broadest sense of the word.] This phrase requires the reader to reach out – to ponder and try harder – to make connections that are more complex than the previous examples.

The dropping of easy conventions, in favour of difficult creative images, requires the reader to apply more energy and work harder to make the connections. In this process the 'sparks' need to leap further between the dendritic kindling.

The use of angels, as a method of describing something divine, is quite old: sings like an angel, plays the violin like an angel, looks like an angel, cooks like an angel. The angel is a long-standing, archetypical convention for excellence and beauty.

But the use of devil's angels modifies that idea of beauty, these angels are obviously sinful beauties. As such, they allude to the pain and rasping friction of their myriad angelic feet, as they gyrate on the dance floor of the tongue.

This is a more intricate fusion of images; therefore, I think it is more creative, and more difficult to grasp, than previous examples. The creativity in the descriptions is becoming more concentrated.

LEVEL FIVE.

Eating these chillies is like having a thousand drunken angels dance the fandango on my tongue – in stilettos.

I am holding onto the conventions of angels as an archetype of beauty and excellence. This time the devil reference is dropped in favour of an absurd numerical allusion. Its precision suggests someone might have counted them, which presents an amusing pedantry missing from previous descriptions.

The fact the angels are drunk introduces a mischievous element to the image, suggesting these are not conventional angels. Plus, the reference to the fandango adds a new dimension: the extravagant features of the dance can be used as a metaphor for an argument, a boisterous event or celebratory behaviour. And in the final words a sexual allusion has entered... on tiptoe.

Stiletto heels may well symbolise the taste of chilli, as an exotic – perhaps even erotic– dangerous and physically stimulating experience.

Many chilli-eating aficionados report they receive an endorphin rush from the experience of eating chillies, which adds to their enjoyment – even making the chillies addictive. Perhaps, the revelation of this aspect of the experience refers to previously missed facet of the meal.

A number of questions are rising as I hack my way through the neural forest. Is there a growing detail to the description – even though the language appears more vague and less specific?

Does the abstraction of the experience allow a freedom – inviting the reader to bring their own images and feelings to the experience?

Are these freedoms absent when the description is unequivocal and prescriptive?

In my attempts to be more creative, have I moved from being didactic to being less instructive?

Am I sliding from the external to the internal?

Am I moving from objective to the subjective; perhaps from the scientific to the artistic?

Does this suggest convention 'sides' with science?

Does this mean science is simply a catalogue of conventions we all agree upon?

Do these characteristics make the description more entertaining, more challenging, more fulfilling?

Ultimately, do these abstract properties make the description more creative and more concentrated?

LEVEL SIX.

Eating the chillies crashes a taste car into my tongue wall – too young, too fast. My eyes spontaneously combust, as the safety bag of molten glass and battery acid detonate.

This description moves the experience of eating chillies further away from the conventions of taste. I have invented the bizarre images of a 'taste car' and a 'tongue wall' to describe the chilli eating experience. These are new departures from the previous descriptions– and much more innovative.

They solve the communication problem in a new and more entertaining fashion than previous attempts. In an effort to be more creative, I have described the experience as a real event, using surreal phrases to convey the situation. But have I strayed into hyperbole in an attempt to be more creative?

Is hyperbole part of the attempt to be more creative, or does it intensify and give a truer rendition of the eating experience? Is this what we do when we are trying to be more creative with an internal problem. Do we try to exaggerate the individual experience with the aim of communicating the personal feelings better?

In the domains of science, are the microscope and the telescope devices of hyperbolic investigation? When being creative, do we metaphorically shout louder [or look closer] in the hope the experience is heard sharper? Seen clearer? Perceived better?

In my attempts to explore the unknown, am I sacrificing accuracy in an attempt to be more creative? Or, does attempting to be more creative make the experience richer and ultimately more truthful?

I feel I am behaving like a crime scene investigator, pulling apart the fibres of the description, investigating the micro-fluff and DNA evidence, in an attempt to get at the truth of the experience. When I find something of worth, I turn it into words and show it to the world. Perhaps my hyperbole is the result of my enforced scrutiny of the experience; maybe it is the result of employing higher-intensity creative behaviour.

The ambiguous allusions to young death, invoke images of James Dean, Marilyn Monroe, Jimi Hendrix, along with the prurient frisson of celebrity scandal.

Indirect references are allowed to rise from the purposely vague insinuation. I have invented these purely to communicate, entertain, and search for something fresh and new – something that is an *unconventional* way of representing the eating experience.

This description alludes to something quite outside the eating event. It promotes a connection between the dangers of speed and the hazard of eating the chillies, inferring accidents and explosive sensations.

These painful images are complemented by the references to anguish and heat, as I hit the 'taste windscreen' and my eyes spontaneously combust.

Imagining the horrific shock of being splashed with molten glass and battery acid increases the visceral sensations, and it expresses the feelings of burning skin that accompany eating hot chillies.

Furthermore, we can identify an indirect reference to the anticipation that occurs before the act of eating. A narrative of events has been fashioned to describe the variety of the taste experience.

In this description, we can imagine the expectation as we accelerate at extreme speed, before finally hitting 'the tongue wall' and experiencing the cataclysmic taste.

Consequently, we can identify a new dimension to the description: a timeline. The experience starts in one time and place, then concludes elsewhere. A cinematic element has been introduced to the experience.

I have moved from describing a single incident, to describing a sequence of events – however fleeting.

It appears, as the descriptions becomes more creative, they describe richer and more complex experiences. In addition, I have moved further from the explicit and closer to the implicit.

I am moving further away from the light of convention and deeper into the dark of the unknown.

LEVEL SEVEN.

Eating these chillies is like re-entering earth's atmosphere, strapped to a dentist chair, whilst having a cast of my alimentary canal made from liquid bronze.

The planet is so beautiful from here....

"Where's Tom Hanks when you need him, and Neil and Buzz and Major Tom? Can you here me Major Tom?"

I think Tarquin Vesuvius spends his time at this level.

The descriptions are getting sillier, more ludicrous – laboured and longer. But is it a more creative description? Whatever our divergent feelings about the description, we must focus on the creativity. Is there any reason why creativity is not allowed to be silly, ludicrous, laboured and indulgent? We must stick to the main question: is this description more creative than the previous one? Does the description solve the problem of communicating the chilli eating experience with more inventiveness? Is it exploring the chilli eating experience in ways that were previously unknown? Does it solve the problem by using ideas and phrases that are less conventional?

The description does not read as slickly as previous options, and it is certainly not as contained. However, this lack of polish can be viewed as a further push into the darkness. Perhaps I am intuitively attempting to reflect the discomfort and fragmented quality of the eating experience.

The 'ragged-edged' prose can be seen as an attempt to play with the writing style, with the aim of finding a new perspective.

The cinematic dimension, I noted in an earlier submission, is augmented by reference to popular song imagery, making a richer collection of allusions. The alliteration, I used in an earlier submission, has given way to a more disjointed and scattered description, in an attempt to differentiate between the details of the experience.

The image of the dentist chair suggests the fear and concerns that attend sitting in one, but it also refers to the very real feeling of constriction that the treatment chair brings. Once I have eaten the chillies, I cannot stop the experience until it has run its course. The chillies are entering my body and I cannot set myself free, all I can do is hold onto the arms of the metaphorical 'taste chair'.... and hope. The depiction of a cast being taken of my alimentary canal is hyperbole, reflecting the unnatural burning sensation that accompany the eating experience. This is complemented by a new and different phrase: *the planet is so beautiful from here'*. This expression documents my exhilarating feelings about the event; it places the reader in my eye, experiencing the euphoric state of my mind.

The seemingly bizarre reference to Tom Hanks flitted across my mind canopy, internally charged by the phrase, *'re-entering earth's atmosphere'*. This is a reference to the film, *'Apollo 13'*, and alludes to the tensions and emotions that accompany parts of that cinematic experience.

Neil and Buzz refer to the first moonwalk, and infer an otherworldly comparison between that event and eating chillies. Major Tom is a reference to David Bowie's song 'Space Oddity'. The mis-spelling of 'hear' for 'here' is a [perhaps too obscure] reference to the word play used in the song. Taken together, the space images allude to an unearthly, extreme, elated, sublime emotional and physical chilli eating experience.

We can see the references are becoming more vague and less direct, more implicit and less explicit, which I think makes the description more interesting. However, at the same time, the ambiguity makes the references more obscure and more difficult to access.

Notably, I appear to be striving to satisfy my individual desire to communicate the precision of what I am experiencing in my 'synaptic jungle', rather than searching for a common, shared experience, that I imagine the reader may identify with. I have stopped tramping the well-lit ground of common knowledge. I have wandered into dark territory that has not been explored before.

In that process, some readers may get lost in the undergrowth. But – if the creativity is successful – others may benefit from being party to a richer, and more meaningful exploration.

I think I am exploring places the reader and myself have not been before. I have stopped worrying whether I am making sense, or making contact with the reader.

If I am going to render this experience with honesty, I have to concentrate on **my** experiences and not worry about the sensibilities of the imagined reader.

I am shifting from making easy contact with the audience [which is cliché], towards making effective contact with my own [often unique] thoughts and feelings. In the process, I am also becoming more indulgent. I am moving away from 'communal right' and towards 'individual truth'. I am moving deeper into the creativity zone; it is getting darker in here. I have to try harder to find the true description. The intensity level of my creativity is rising. I am using much more time and energy to wheedle out the essence of the experience. This is the most concentrated creativity, so far.

The further away my 'distribution synapses' are from the readers 'receiving synapses', the further the 'neural spark' has to leap. Consequently, more energy is required to decode the message. Accordingly, the louder and more notable the 'crack' will be when the energy leaps from one jungle 'eco-system' to the next.

Now, there are furry animals skipping around the mind canopy; they are starting to scream and chatter. Many axonic twigs and leaves fall to the floor, but many more seeds develop and begin to grow.

LEVEL EIGHT.

In the restaurant sat a man with no head. On the table, in front of him, is a sign.

NO MORE

CHILLI

PEPPERS.

BY ORDER OF

THE FIRE

DEPARTMENT.

This should cause some readers a problem in its comprehension. Some might think of it as stupid, silly or infantile. Now I am using signposts, to refer to allusions, to wave a stick at the experience.

The surreal nature of the image calls to [my] mind Rene Magritte's paintings, black and white photographs of industrial accidents, or images of peculiar gangster executions.

It suggests another form of the chilli eating experience. It is a warning of the dire consequences of eating chillies. But it is all a little playful: the description cannot be believed to be a factual rendition of the experience.

The notion of a precise depiction of the experience, has been discarded in favour of a stark, visual image – a neural achromatic painting – that can be pored over and 'read' in many different ways. It is rejecting the convention of delivering the message through description. The eating experience is being carried in an obtuse minimalist statement.

Now, I am moving deeper into the dark. I am slipping loose the bonds of convention. I have stopped trying to describe the event for the benefit of the reader. I have stopped looking to easy communal references to heat and spice, or to similes and metaphors of those experiences. I am trying to communicate something that is much more personal, unique and entertaining; this is less mind, more viscera: gut not brain.

LEVEL NINE.

There is a bed somewhere

in intensive care...

Soft pillows,

pulled blinds,

shuffle shoes.

No visitation.

Nil by mouth.

Reserved....

for those that try.

This level of creativity vaults the eating experience into some indeterminate time after the consumption. It rejects the convention of describing the taste, and the process of eating. It takes the narrative straight to the final lines of the final page.

The narrative has gone; the event is implied.

The neural painting is more finely drawn, but now there are crafted smudges and blurs – and less tonal contrast.

This description makes no reference to taste, and there is no suggestion of chilli peppers; consequently, it stretches the imagination of the reader further than the level eight. In addition, there is more innovation in the form of the writing. The description is in the form of a prose poem. The presentation has been played with, in an effort to access another level of creativity.

The use of different font sizes communicates the various intensities of the experience, describing a diminution followed by a crescendo. Now, each line or phrase is an anodyne, soft-focus image, strung together into a soothing analgesic exhibition. Finally, the last words are written in italics, using the smallest font, perhaps symbolising an ambiguous, plaintive whisper that elicits the question, "What should not be tried?"

At the same time, the description alludes to trenches poetry: it appears to be an elegy, a requiem – to those that eat chillies. It uses the short sentence of funeral ovation and hints at imminent death. Or perhaps, the impending recovery of life?

Do the exaggerated claims heighten the chilli eating experience? Does this account express the experience more clearly? Or, does the report make the description more entertaining?

At the same time as I concentrate on my own very personal experience, I am inviting the reader to join me in my indulgence: in my attempt to find, a new pathway, a new connection.... a new, or improved, solution to the communication problem.

It seems, rather than solving problems for the reader, I am posing the reader problems. I am moving away from didacticism. I have stopped telling the reader what to think and how to interpret the experience. I am requiring the reader to bring their own dish to the feast, so they can draw upon, and examine, their own conventions. In this way, the relationship is changing. The descriptions are more collaborative and democratic, perhaps more nourishing.

I think this change makes the later descriptions more creative. Some of the images are coming from me. But also, many are expected from the mind of the reader. The description has become a team event, in which the writer and the reader converge on a meaning.

But this is always the way: a conventional description would employ phrases and ideas we have all learnt to agree upon. Conventions are communications that convey meanings that have already been converged upon. Hot, spicy, burning, are broad communal images and experiences symbolised in words.

New, creative images are different. These images are less communal, less homogenous, more personal and individual. They are written out in spidery long hand, like squiggly, gangling mycelium.

If they are to become conventions, we have to work at them. We need to repeat them, fatten them up, so we can understand them and learn their meanings. We need to render them strong, safe, proven and known. We need to turn them into shorthand symbols of convention. We need to block them in with mops and brooms, with purple paint, on bill boards. They have to become stout branches in the communal synaptic forest that we can all swing from.

This is what happens in the human learning experience. We take the unknown and we turn it into the known. We take the low-benefit creative product, and we turn it into high-benefit creative product, and then into a convention. We do this by learning about it, assimilating it, and passing it on to others.

LEVEL TEN.

Anticipation...................hot debate

WoW!–NapAlm soup- Joan of Arc [welding]

cRAcK-a-Toe-Ahh- to the nose cone of

9/11 acid, tears of the mother- shingles of the tongue,

NAGASAKI- heeeeeeerrrre....

heeet- ApollOh! Oh! Oh! 13-

Alimentaryafterburn-BURNfactor 5 0 h! book him Donnoh! Oh! Oh!

RED wHOT? POKERS.........

EDDIE second......eddie 2.....too much, ooh, ooh, ooh!

The rejection of the convention of sentences and punctuation, combined with seemingly nonsensical and indiscriminate use of capitals, suggest an experience that is only just holding onto the convention of words, writing.... let alone eating.

This is a stream of thought, or a vented steam of ideas. These are images devoid of many of the conventions of written or spoken language. The mis-spelt names and words convey a disjointed, mind challenging experience, where the images form a puzzle in need of deciphering.

Because of the ambiguity, the reader has to work hard to make the connections. Then the reader is required to transpose the images into a meaningful representation of the experience. Now the neural painting has given way to a neural collage, or combination of images, that suggest experiences of gustatory heat and burning.

The painting has daubed ideas on the page, to be made sense of in the head of the reader's chemical synaptic eco-system. The disjointed, staccato, 'splash-narrative' rejects the convention of linear description.

This all culminates in the euphoric, jumble-emotion reference to Edward the Second and an allusion to the myth of his unpleasant death. The play with spellings and fonts, suggests the ecstatic hyperbolic state of disarray that can accompany eating something so hot and spicy that it jangles the thoughts and feelings. The abstract expressionistic process sends the mind and body reeling.

LEVEL ELEVEN.

A scale from one to ten must have a level eleven.

Now the umbilical cord of convention is completely severed. Just like Major Tom, we are drifting – looking for something firm to hook ourselves to – but we can find nothing but empty space.

A very good example of level eleven creativity might describe eating the chilli as a collection of expletives, arranged as anagrams, interspersed with instructions on how to change the brake pads on a Porsche, sung in Portuguese.

There appears to be no connection between the description and the event. But there is an interesting thing about this level of creativity. Although this level seems incomprehensible and removed from reality, once we try to decipher the description – if we try hard enough – if we use enough high-intensity creative behaviour, and we *believe* there is a sincere connection, we can find one – however tenuous. Just as we can find cities in the clouds and monsters in the shadows.

The level eleven creative product becomes our own Rorschach Test. We can find meaning in anything, if we believe there is one there, if we look hard enough, and we have a problem that needs solving. In other words, we bring our internal thoughts and perceptions to bear upon our external environment and experiences.

At level eleven, I am only trying to make minimal contact. If there is a meaning to the communication, it happens almost totally through the imagination of the reader.

However bizarre the description may appear, with the application of the reader's tenacious thoughts, and their determination to make sense of what they are experiencing, it is possible for them to find some personal meaning in the creative product.

All I have done is supplied a shapeless set of images, and prompted the reader to find the connection. The receiver overlays the 'arbitrary' creative product with meaning that comes from their own imagination and their own problems. Like some arcane cryptologist trying to make sense of esoteric encoded messages, we try to make sense of what, at first sight, appears to be nonsensical. In that process we reveal our innermost thoughts, feelings and problems, as we search our most remote innate conventions for a meaningful sign.

Level eleven provides a blank canvas – a clean slate – so the reader can pick and project their own images. This most abstruse description allows a search of our innermost problems and most hidden human experiences. Level eleven provides a strange dream that requires interpretation, re-ordering, and rendering sensible by the reader.

Finding patterns and sense in the obscure is a very human property, sometimes used by psychologists to examine the workings of a patient's thoughts. It is also used in the presentations of charlatans that 'read' the minds of the gullible, and in the work of a whole range of artists that are attempting to tap into a common primal experience.

LEVEL UULL.

Unfortunately, level eleven is a convention. Many will recognise the inclusion as a reference to a scene from the spoof documentary '*Spinal Tap*'. Once, this was a high-benefit creative product; now, it is a time-honoured convention.

I cannot abide a convention at the extreme end of a creativity spectrum, so I am going to create a level twelve, but this would continue the convention of using numbers to differentiate between contents of a list. Therefore, I am going to rename level twelve 'Uull' which is an anagram of 'Lulu' which is the name of a dog: a particularly fine and 'off the wall' dog.

This is the highest concentration of creativity I can conceive. Essentially, level Uull dispenses with all conventions. Uull is such high-level creativity nobody else gets it, not even me – and I am proposing it.

I think I did get it once, but the thought was so sublime and unattainable it dissolved moments after I had it. It makes the description of the chillies experience so bizarre, so supremely incomprehensible, it makes the creative thought condense into a transient whirling arctic blast in my neural plantation.

Ultimately, Uull is a fleeting idea, an electrochemical transmission that failed in the leap. It is the oily notion that could not grasp the next branch, so it 'earths' in the bark, the leaves and the buds. Uull is a mystery that cannot be articulated: an invitation to faith, perhaps from the divine.

We've all had these Uull thoughts. Often at times when we are desperately trying to solve a problem. Then, whilst looking the wrong way– or whilst in the middle of a tweedling conversation– something sublime 'pops' into the head, glazing the eyes, and forcing the examination of a crack in the ceiling, or a stain on the floor.

Before you can write it down – or tell anyone else – it dissolves into an absurd mutter, or changes into a pattern on the wall .... or a flatulent smile. It is like finding a magnificent long wanted solution, for which there is no problem. Perhaps it is the answer to an unrecognised puzzle. Uull is untainted, undiluted creativity. At the moment of Uull, I am experiencing the zenith of creativity. A point that is impossible to communicate to others. Level Uull is an expression of the supreme low-benefit creative product.

Lost in the darkness of the creativity zone, with no compass to aid return, I cannot reach anyone else, or make sense. There is no language, and no existing domain, that could convey what I am experiencing. I am connecting with the lone, supreme, transitory being: me. I am answerable to no one. I can think and imagine what I like, without restriction or concern for anyone else. Here is creativity in its purest form.... without encumbrance of any convention. I am my own god, in my own individual universe, with no one to question, or interfere – no need for communication. No need for explanation.

No need to make sense.

Like a child waiting for birth.

3.12. THE EXTREMES OF THE QUALITY SPECTRUM.

We could, if we wish, disregard level eleven and level Uull as beyond creativity – as the approach to some form of psychosis. But I think we could agree that the incremental order of the rest of the descriptions is sound.

A good test of this would be to write the descriptions on pieces of card then try to put them in order of creativity, with the least creative first and the most creative last. Would an impartial observer put them in the same order as I have presented them? There may be some ear-tugging and discussion, even argument, but I think the order would remain the same.

I think we could create similar spectrums of creativity for other domains. How about a creativity spectrum for beds, bicycles, birthday cakes, hats, portraits, flower arrangements, political manifestoes?

I think we could, and should, create a spectrum of creativity for every domain. It could be stored and curated online: **Creative Spectrums.com** [*Or perhaps we could call it something a little more creative.*]

It would be a wonderful focus for discussion, and a useful depository of creative thought. The more spectrums we created, and the more similarities we could observe, the closer we would come to understanding the nature of creativity.

Also, we would become much more familiar with the qualities we use to explore the vast unknown.

If we can agree about the creative order of the chilli eating descriptions, we can progress to making some observations about the qualities of the spectrum.

My first observation is, the more creative a description is the more absurd it becomes.

And so, the first spectrum of creative quality would record low-level, but reasonably sensible creativity at one end, and irrational mind-gouging absurdity at the other.

THE QUALITY SPECTRUM OF CREATIVITY

0—1—2—3— 4 — 5 — 6 – 7—8—9—10

LOW-QUALITY -- HIGH-QUALITY
CREATIVITY   CREATIVITY

Sensible   Absurd

From this observation, we can state there is a solid link between absurdity and creativity.

In other words, the highest concentrations of creativity have the highest concentrations of absurdity.

With this paradigm established, we can look for other spectrums that may help our identification and understanding of creativity.

EASY – DIFFICULT

First attempts at describing the chilli eating experience were easy. I just applied low-intensity creativity to one of the many clichéd observations that we all use when we need an easy and effective communication. As I searched for more interesting, and more creative ways, of describing the experience, the communication required more time and effort from me. And, I assume, more effort from the receiver to understand the communication. This observation reveals low-quality creativity is easy to produce, and make sense of. Higher quality creativity is more difficult to produce, and understand.

SIMPLE – COMPLEX

The lower quality descriptions begin as quite simple expressions, with common references we all understand. But, as the creative behaviour becomes more concentrated, so the descriptions become more complex, more difficult to interpret and make sense of.

PRECISION – AMBIGUITY

The descriptions move from the precision of easy-to-understand low-level creativity at one end of the spectrum to ambiguity at the higher levels. The ambiguity reflects the imprecision found when working in the dark of the unknown. Many statements at the higher end of the quality spectrum are half-guesses and 'stabs in the dark'. Lower-level creativity contains more known elements; higher quality creativity contains more unknown elements.

BROAD – DETAILED

My first attempts at creativity are broad in their descriptions; the latter, more creative, descriptions are more detailed and comprehensive, uncovering aspects of the experience I had missed or ignored in previous examples. As I raised the intensity of my creative behaviour, I noticed my tendency to search for specifics that could provide a more interesting and nuanced description of the eating experience.

LOW-INTENSITY / HIGH-INTENSITY

As the intensity of my creative behaviour increased, so did the concentration of my creative behaviour. With more intensity I became more penetrating and particular. I picked apart smaller and smaller parts of the problem in an attempt to get closer to a solution. With more intensity, I attempted a more diverse examination of the problems structure. The more I searched, the more I saw.

PLAIN – RICH

The lower quality descriptions appear to be quite plain in their construction, language and ideas; the latter, higher quality descriptions appear richer in meaning.

COMMUNAL – PERSONAL

This was a very noticeable attribute of the spectrum. As the descriptions became more creative, I observed I was trying to get to the essence of my personal experience, I realised I was slowly releasing myself from caring about the communal experience.

I was removing the 'communal blocks' that require me to communicate and make sense to the reader. I was closing in on my private thoughts and feelings. I was moving away from the desire to connect with other people.

I was moving towards a need to connect with the truth of my own experiences. I stopped caring about the audience's expectations, as I searched for a personal, unique and incisive response.

INCLUSIVE – EXCLUSIVE

The solutions of the lower quality descriptions are inclusive: they appear to solve the communication problem for a much larger constituency.

In contrast, the higher quality creative descriptions appear to be relevant to an increasingly smaller collection of people.

The higher quality, more concentrated creative, descriptions tend to exclude others from the communication.

ADHERENCE TO FORM – PLAY WITH FORM

In an attempt to be more creative, I studied and played with all aspects of the problem; one of the most fundamental features was the form of the description.

I moved from compliance with the conventions of the form, at level zero, to outright destruction and refusal to use conventions at the higher end of the spectrum.

UNIMAGINATIVE – IMAGINATIVE

Low-quality, dilute creativity, requires little imagination from the reader to understand. As I progress to the higher quality creativity, the reader is required to employ increasingly higher levels of imagination in an effort to make sense of the description and form meaningful understandings.

MUNDANE – MYSTERIOUS

The further I move into the darkness of the creativity zone, the more mysterious and less mundane the descriptions become. As I move away from the light of conventions, the higher levels of creative behaviour require the stretching of old sensibilities and the propagation of new ones.

In the darkness of the unknown, I lack satisfactory 'stock' vocabulary or phrases to express myself, so I have to experiment, and make up more previously unused, and therefore mysterious, forms that have not been tried before.

OBVIOUS – OBSCURE

The descriptions move from the obvious, at the lower levels of creativity, to the obscure at the higher levels. As I attempt to find new ways of communicating new experiences, I have to play with new ways of describing the event.

****

264

SYNTHESIS

From the ten descriptions and 'opposite sets' of words, we can synthesise a list of adjectives.

At the lower levels of the creativity quality spectrum, we find mundane, sensible, easy, boring, simple, precise, explicit, broad, obvious, low-intensity, inclusive, as well as playing to audience, and an adherence to form. These adjectives describe the lower quality, more dilute, creative products.

And we can create another list to describe higher quality creative products: absurdity, mysterious, play with form, exclusivity, personal, detailed, obscure, vague, complex, implicit and difficult. These adjectives describe the higher expressions of creativity.

Armed with these adjectives as our criteria, could we decide if one creative product employed more concentrated creative behaviour than another creative product?

Would it be possible to identify high, medium or low-quality creativity in a collection of creative products?

Could we, with a fair wind and a clear sky, claim a certain creative product shows level three creative behaviour, and that another creative product deserves to be located at level eight?

I think we could.

And could we use the spectrum to improve our creativity?

Again, I think we could.

For example, if a level two creative product fails to solve a problem, we may use information gleaned from the spectrum to apply higher levels of creativity. We could use behaviours linked to the adjectives to attempt to go further into the darkness of the unknown. These higher qualities of creativity may solve our problem.

But it should be noted the concentration of creativity in a creative product, by itself, is largely immaterial to its problem-solving abilities. As we have seen elsewhere, when applying creative behaviour, the only thing we are really interested in is the ability for the creative product to solve the problem – not on how creative it is. Once a problem is solved there is no point in continuing to solve it. When engaged in problems solving, it is irrelevant whether we use level two creativity, level seven creativity or absurd Uull.

Creativity is simply a method for finding ways to solve our problems when our conventions are inadequate or have failed us. The aim of creative behaviour is to solve the problem, not to be creative. Higher concentrated creativity does not necessarily result in a better solution. We must be careful not to make being creative our goal; the goal must always be solving the problem.

These spectrums, and their polar adjectives, are useful tools in our quest to understand creativity. They provide a language we can use to communicate with each other about this vital behaviour, and they allow us to identify ways we can improve and direct our creative behaviours in our effort to solve our problems and analyse our efforts.

3.13. THE EXTREMES OF THE PROBLEM-SOLVING SPECTRUM.

Having examined the extremes of the quality spectrum of creativity, we now possess further insight to help us understand the phenomenon of creative behaviour. But we can go further: if we take the quality spectrum of creativity and combine it with the circle of conventions, we can create the full spectrum of problem-solving behaviour. This spectrum encompasses all of our behaviours. From the most innate conventions, at the centre of the circle, to the most absurd creativity of Uull, in the furthest reaches of our unknown.

The Circle of Conventions-including the Quality Spectrum of Creativity.

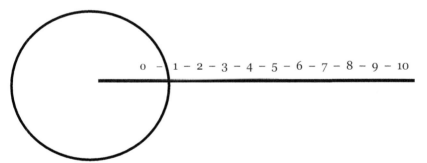

By identifying the outermost reaches of the spectrum [at 10] we can recognise the broad spread of our problem-solving behaviour.

From the most ancient and essential convention, to the highest most absurd creative product.

Once again, it should be noted that many of these 'opposite sets' of words are related to each other and are close partners.

Often they overlap; or they are slightly different expressions of similar characteristics. This should not be a problem. Indeed, their similarities should help our understanding. By using different words to describe these qualities, and by approaching them from an alternative angle, we sometimes reveal a nuance of meaning which can provide added insight.

Many of these extremes have already been exposed in previous chapters, so I will not comment upon them with too much detail.

PAST–FUTURE.

At the centre of the circle of conventions are the creative products of the extreme past. These have become the most dependable and essential problems solving behaviours. We rely upon these base conventions for our existence.

To the right of the spectrum are the most modern experimental attempts at problem solving. It is in our problem-solving creativity that our future is found. We rely upon this creativity for our future.

ANSWERS – QUESTIONS.

The circle of conventions represents the answers we have already found to our problems. The creativity end of the spectrum represents the answers we need to find if we are to understand and expand the control of our environment.

Therefore, conventions deal with answers creativity deals with questions.

268

SMALL ENVIRONMENT – LARGE ENVIRONMENT.

The centre of the circle depicts a time when we had a much smaller understanding of our environment. The right of the spectrum represents the largest and widest conception of our environment. The extreme right of creativity has the potential to extend the boundaries of our environment.

CALM – TURBULENT.

Conventional solutions are easy to accept. If we adopt the convention, we choose the calm and easy route, which is agreeable to our community and assured to work.

At the other end of the spectrum, creativity is challenging and restless. Creative behaviour is often turbulent.

SPECIES – INDIVIDUAL.

The extreme left of the spectrum represents the behaviour all of our species uses. The extreme right of the spectrum represents the behaviour of the individual.

The individual is the starting point of all creativity; the individual is a bearer of the new idea that has the potential to be copied by others and go on to improve the lives of the rest of the species.

SUCCESS – FAILURE.

Ancient conventions are the essence of successful behaviour. These behaviours have been tried and tested over many generations and always work.

Indeed, they are essential for life to succeed. However, the more creative our behaviour becomes the more likely we are to experience failure. Failure is found outside of the circle of conventions. This is where we examine new problems, and experiment with new behaviour that is untested. Creativity always has the potential to fail.

EARLY EVOLUTION– FUTURE EVOLUTION.

The centre of the circle represents the earliest forms of convention. It is here our chemical and biological solutions, along with and our earliest behaviours, were created. These are the earliest deposits in our catalogue of conventions, and the earliest contributions to our evolution. Behaviour that is closer to the circumference of the circle represents more recent expressions of creativity. Behaviour that falls outside of the circle represents future potential creations that may one day become our conventions and contribute to the future evolution of our species.

NORMAL – ABNORMAL.

Normal behaviour [the behaviour of the majority] is located inside the circle of conventions. The closer our behaviour is to the centre of the circle of convention, the more normal or natural it is considered to be by the majority.

The closer behaviour gets to the circumference of the less normal it may appear to the majority. The behaviour that happens outside of the circle is often labelled as abnormal.

All conventional behaviour, we use today, was once abnormal behaviour. If abnormal behaviour is eventually seen as beneficial to others, it becomes adopted as a convention and absorbed into the circle of convention.

STATUS QUO – CHANGE.

The behaviour located in the circle of conventions represents the status quo and are the foundations of our lives. These solutions have been tried and tested over a long time, and found to be efficient and dependable.

In contrast, outside of the circle, in the darkness of the unknown, is the place that change is constantly happening. This is where life changing questions swirl and take form. This is the place where new challenges are conceived and accepted.

From this we can confirm that conventions are the status quo and creativity is the agent of change.

SAFE – RISKY.

Conventional behaviour is very safe. However, the implementation of a creative product is potentially a risky experiment.

Creative behaviour is untried, untested – and can be dangerous.

How dangerous the creativity is, depends upon the domain that the creativity is taking place in, and the level of creative behaviour that is engaged in.

EXPERT – NOVICE.

We can make a claim for conventions as the home of the expert and expertise. The expert is someone that knows every convention of a domain. But as we have seen, to be creative we have to question our conventions. We have to reconsider what we know, and what we value. We need to propose new ideas and new creative products that may interrogate and challenge our conventions. Often, the expert clings to convention and rejects creativity. Often, the creative novice is ignorant of conventions.

SOLID – FLUID.

Conventional behaviours are solid and can be the most resolute and difficult behaviours to alter. Our oldest conventions are set in our bones and our blood, they are the most difficult, if not impossible, to change. These early conventional behaviours are solidly set in our characters and are rarely examined or challenged.

At the other end of the spectrum, outside of the circle, our creative behaviours are open to change and play. Creative behaviours are fluid and mutable.

BORING – EXCITING.

Creativity excites people: new creative products arouse the interest of people and encourage investigation, stimulating them to think, challenging them to change their behaviours and lives. Conventions are part of the solid structure of behaviour, they are expected and they are dependable, rarely are they exciting. Conventions are boring.

RIGHT – WRONG.

A convention is the 'right' answer to an old problem. Creativity is constantly getting it wrong. We are constantly using creativity to try new ideas, twisting them around and struggling with them to find new solutions and improving existing ones.

COMMON – RARE.

Our oldest conventions represent common behaviour, everybody uses these solutions. Creativity represents a small proportion of our behaviour; creativity is rare behaviour.

LOW ENERGY – HIGH ENERGY.

Conventions use the least amount of energy to solve a problem. Creativity frequently uses a lot of time and energy. Often, we have to work hard and use lots of energy to find creative solutions that make our lives longer and better, or improve upon the conventions of a domain.

FOUNDATIONS – PEAKS.

Conventional behaviour is the foundation of the community. Without conventions, creativity would have nothing to build upon, or push away from. Conventions are the rules of the game that creativity attempts to break or change. Creative behaviour is the peak of individualistic behaviour.

HERITAGE – DESTINY.

Our oldest conventions are our heritage. These 'foundation conventions' have driven our evolution. Creativity is built upon old conventions and propels us into the future.

Therefore, our conventions represent our heritage, and creativity represents our destiny.

The problems we recognise, and the ones we decide to solve, are the driving force of our species cultural evolution.

REALITY – DREAMS.

The extreme conventions are the reality of our everyday lives. Our species has created todays lives from billions of creative products, over millions of years. To the extreme right of the spectrum are our future solutions, hidden in the turbulent mystery of the unknown. We create our lives from our imaginations – from the questions we ask and the problems we pose. If we can imagine it, we can turn it into our reality.

KNOWN – UNKNOWN.

Conventions are the sum total of everything we know. When we move beyond the circumference of our circle of conventions, we are entering a space where everything is unknown.

The creativity zone – outside of the circle of conventions – represents what we do not know, and what we do not understand.

When being creative, we are exploring the unknown and the mysterious, we do not know where it is going to lead us, what we might find, or what the repercussions might be.

MORPHOLOGY – MIND.

At one end of the problem-solving spectrum, in the centre of the circle, we have deeply entrenched, cell-deep, sensible convention, and at the other end we have the most contemporary, foggy, creative, absurd mist of 'Uull' thinking.

This is a primary division of the problems solving spectrum, that reinforces a simple fact: present day solid conventions were once the amorphous creative behaviours of the past.

Consequently, we can say that our present-day reality has been made by our past creativity: by the problems our ancestors recognised, the questions they asked, and the choices they made.

SWEET DREAMS

We must take care.

We should be cautious what we wish for.

Our solid conventions were once our wildest thoughts.

Today's granite foundations were once flags and banners.

Today's reveries will become tomorrow's reality.

One day all of our problems will be solved.

One day all our fantasies will come true.

We construct our future with creativity.

We live each day in the dreams of our ancestors...

Let's hope their dreams were sweet.

kjb

3.14. AFTERWORD.

Nothing is complete [yet].

There is always something more to do.

Many aspects of this book expose areas that require further investigation, even revision.

And so, another book is required.

If you wish to contribute your observations, thoughts, questions criticisms or improvements,

please e-mail me at: **kevinjanbonner@hotmail.co.uk.**

My humility knows no bounds.

Similarly, if you wish to contribute a spectrum of creativity, in any domain – please do not hesitate.

I shall endeavour to collate them into some meaningful form at some time in the future.

GLOSSARY & INDEX.

DOMAINS: A collection of behaviours and actions focussed on a human activity. For example, art domains, or music domains. Pg 15

CREATIVE PROCESS: Series of behaviours that are intended to lead to the making of creative product. Pg 27

PRETEND CREATIVITY: Creativity applied to an invented problem. Often used in creativity tests or games. Pg 33

AUTHENTIC CREATIVITY: Creativity applied to a problem that has importance to the person trying to solve the problem. Pg 33

EXAM FACTORY: A pejorative description of schools that are concentrated on passing exams above all else. Pg 46

SELECTIVE ADVANTAGE: Any characteristic, trait or behaviour that gives an organism a greater chance of surviving and reproducing than the available alternatives. Pgs 63/64

VICTORIAN WORK ETHIC: An attitude that claims working hard as a best way to be successful in life. Pg 74

TWO PART CREATIVITY: The idea that creativity needs to be split into two parts in order for it to be analysed and understood, namely, creative behaviour and creative product. Pg 89

LOW-INTENSITY CREATIVE BEHAVIOUR: Creative behaviour that uses small amounts of time and energy to produce a Creative Product. Pg89

THE BENEFIT SPECTRUM OF THE CREATIVE PRODUCT: The graphic depiction of a collection of creative products on a spectrum with low-benefit creative products at one end and high-benefit creative products at the other. Pg 89

LOW-BENEFIT CREATIVE PRODUCT: A creative product that benefits a small number of people– in the extreme one person. Pg 90

HIGH-BENEFIT CREATIVE PRODUCT: The creative product that benefits lots of people–in the extreme the species. Pg 93

THE BENEFIT SPECTRUM SHIFT: The ability for creative products to be relocated on the benefit spectrum in response to changing values. Often high-benefit creative products will over time become low-benefit creative products. Pg 97

SMALL CREATIVE PRODUCTS: Small creative parts of a much larger conventional construction. Pg 211

MALCREATIVITY: Creativity that produces unpleasant outcomes. Pg 101

AHA! MOMENT: The creative idea that comes to mind in an instant, often when least expected. Pg 106

MORAL SPECTRUM OF CREATIVITY: The graphic depiction of creative products with focus on their morality. At one end is creative products that everyone thinks is bad, at the other end is products that everyone thinks is good. Pgs 104/109

EPHEMERAL CREATIVITY: Creativity that results products that are high-benefit for a short period of time. Pg 111/210/ 186

FAILED CREATIVITY: Creative behaviour that fails to find a successful creative product. Sometimes it is the things learnt from the failure that remain as the creative product. Pgs 113/145.

EXTERNAL CREATIVITY: Creativity that deals with problems that emanate from the 'real' world – things that we all experience. As opposed to the 'internal' world of our individual minds. External creativity is associated with problems of Science/Discovery/External, and often can be objectively assessed. Pg 133.

INTERNAL CREATIVITY: Creativity that deals with problems that emanate from the internal world of our minds. Problems that experienced internally, as opposed to the problems of the external world. Internal creativity is associated with Art/Invention. Pg 133

PRIMARY CREATIVITY: Creativity that was used by early Mankind to deal with the real problems of survival. Pg 136

SECONDARY CREATIVITY: Creativity that was used by later Mankind that dealt with more internal problems, often producing entertainment and art. Pg 140

TERTIARY CREATIVITY: Creativity used by more modern Mankind that examines more complex personal problems. Pg 140

BRIEFED CREATIVITY: Creativity that is driven by a brief- often used in the world of design and business. Pg 208/149

SPECTRUM OF PROBLEMS: Graphic depiction of problems encountered by Mankind. Easy problems are located at one end of the spectrum complex difficult problems at the other. Pgs 153/208

CONVENTIONS: Solutions to problems that are inherited or learnt. Sometimes thought of as the status quo. Pg 157 et al.

INNATE CONVENTIONS: Conventions that have been passed on from parents genetically at birth. Pg 158

LEARNT CONVENTIONS: Conventions acquired since birth. Pg 159

THE CIRCLE OF CONVENTIONS: Graphic representation of the total conventions available to an individual or group of people. Pg 163

THE CREATIVITY ZONE: Graphic representation of the space, outside of the convention circle. Pg 169

CREATIVE INNOCENCE: Early childhood: a time in our lives before we had learnt conventions. Pg 176

TARQUIN VESUVIUS: Fictional character, invented to explore the life of someone that is permanently creative. Pgs 56/173/181

THE ESSENTIAL PROBLEM: The problem that has to be in existence [but not necessarily noticed] for creative behaviour to take place. Pg 185

THE CREATIVE PRODUCT: The result of creative behaviour.Pgs 93/189

THE LAW OF DIMINISHING RETURNS: A law borrowed from Economics: in this context it refers to the way that the more exposure to a creative product a person has, the less benefit the person attributes to that product. Pg 201

THE QUALITY SPECTRUM OF CREATIVITY: Graphic depiction of creative products that focusses on creative quality. Low-quality creative products are located at one end of the spectrum, high-quality creative products are located at the other end. Pg 221/258

LEVEL UULL: Level Uull is the highest level of creative quality 255

NOTES..........

Printed in Great Britain
by Amazon

83850930R00169